HIGH
TICKET
REVOLUTION

Adam Cerra

HIGH TICKET REVOLUTION

From Zero to $ix Figures
A Closer's Journey to Wealth

ISBN: 9798854669450

Imprint: Independently published

This book was produced in collaboration with Write Business Results Limited. For more information on their business book, blog and podcast services, please visit www.writebusinessresults.com or contact the team via info@writebusinessresults.com.

Acknowledgments

I would like to take a moment to express my deepest gratitude to my loving wife. Her unwavering support, understanding, and encouragement have been the bedrock of my successful career in high-ticket sales. Her belief in me, even during challenging times, has fueled my determination to excel.

I am incredibly thankful for the individuals who have played a significant role in shaping my journey. To my mentors and coaches, your guidance and wisdom have been invaluable. Your belief in my potential and your willingness to share your knowledge and experiences have greatly contributed to my growth and achievements.

I am also indebted to my team. Your collaboration, camaraderie, and shared commitment to my high-ticket agency have created an environment conducive to success.

To my clients, I extend my heartfelt appreciation. Your trust, loyalty, and willingness to invest in my high-ticket agency have not only contributed to my professional success, but have also allowed me to witness firsthand the transformative power of our services.

Lastly, I would like to express my gratitude to the industry experts and thought leaders whose insights and innovative approaches have inspired and shaped my career. Your contributions have broadened my perspective and enhanced my ability to deliver exceptional results.

To all those who have believed in me, supported me, and contributed to my successful career in the high-ticket industry, I am eternally grateful. Your impact on my professional journey is immeasurable, and I cherish the relationships and experiences we have shared.

Thank you,
Adam Cerra

Contents

Foreword

Want the perfect "close"? Of course you do – we all want that.

I've met and trained 80,000+ salespeople and most of them get excited by new ideas, but when it came down to doing any prep work, well, they just wanted an "easy button" to lock-in more sales and commissions.

Unfortunately, there's no easy button – no matter how many funnels or scripts you build or what kind of "AI" you use.

Want the good news?

In the pages of Adam's book are exciting and effective methods that will work in today's crazily competitive sales world.

Adam Cerra has discovered one of the newest methods of selling, and put it down word by word for you to read, consume, follow and… use.

This book shows very clearly why everything your competition is doing will just confuse the customer, and leave them frustrated.

So, all you have to do is step in, and do something so simple – and Adam explains just how simple. By doing that unexpected thing, patterns are broken, emotions are ignited, conversations are started, ideas are exchanged… and sales are made.

This book has my earnest endorsement and it's certainly time for you to throw out "99 Effective Closes" or whatever else is occupying dead space on your bookshelf, and put this book in its place.

Adam's methodology works, and works fast.

Oren Klaff
Bestselling author of *'Pitch Anything'* and *'Flip The Script'*

Mastering the Art of Persuasion

Before we go any further, let me be very clear here – this is not a traditional sales book.

What I'm going to teach you in this book is a career that unlocks the way to six-figure freedom.

This is a career at the heart of a new and thriving industry – all you need to do to get hired and be successful is to commit to mastering the skills laid out in this book. It's a skill set that once you have mastered, you will have with you for the rest of your life and can keep cashing in on.

The 9-5 life is dying

What does a typical day look like for you? How much time do you get to spend doing the things you enjoy with the people you love vs the time you give up to an over-demanding job?

1

I have been a sales expert and trainer for nearly twenty years now. When I look back on my early days, it is shocking how much the job demanded of me. I'd have to leave before my kids were up in the morning, and would only return long after they'd gone to bed. The hours in between were grueling and stress-filled – I'd have to suffer call after call getting cut off before I even finished saying my name.

Back then, I felt I had to live with it. What other options were there, really? The choices were, "Do the work that puts food on the table and keeps a roof over our heads" or, "End up on the streets". A bit of short-term suffering was nothing in comparison.

That was twenty years ago. These days things are very different.

Covid, financial upheaval, and rapid advances in technology are all catalysts which have, over the last few years, been driving a mini-revolution in the workplace. People all of a sudden have a *choice*.

We have tasted the fruit of what it's like working from home; what it's like to have a rewarding career and still be able to spend valuable time with our families. We have seen average Joes pack up and quit their jobs and work wherever the hell they want, doing something they love.

So many people are now taking a proper, deep look at their lives. What they see is employers who don't actually care for them as individuals. Their jobs are often dead-end grinds, working for long hours bashing away at a keyboard long after their friends have clocked out and headed to the bar or their kids have gone to bed. In return for their sacrifices, what do they get? Pennies.

The question they're asking themselves is – what happens if, five years down the line, nothing has changed and I'm still slaving away at that same keyboard long into the evening? Their relationships and their passions all might have withered away without having had the freedom to actually do anything other than work.

What they need is a way out – an escape from the 9–5. A way you can spend time doing something meaningful that adds value to people's lives, all the while working on your own clock.

I know it's possible. Myself, my team, and the people I coach have done it. There is nothing special about us. We are just normal men and women like you who have had enough of the grind. You can be your own boss, work anywhere you want, and have a very comfortable six-figure salary if you read on, and act on what you read.

Now, you might have considered sales. You might have tried it briefly or dismissed it out of hand. It doesn't have to be a job that you do because you couldn't get anything else. The issue is that it doesn't actually feel much better, right? A micromanaging "team leader" tells you to keep making more calls, keep dialing that phone, never take "no" for an answer… ugh. In the end, every interaction with a prospect becomes transactional as you're pushed to find the "perfect" trick or pressure tactic that will push them to buy as quickly as possible.

The thing is, it doesn't have to be like that. It can be so much more – and so much more rewarding. A sales job could actually be an opportunity to grow and develop while helping others. It doesn't have to be an unskilled job that you do just to get by – working your ass off for pennies while everyone else has already clocked off for the day. The key is that we need to take a more professional approach to sales as an industry.

Sales doesn't have to be manipulative and selling people things they don't want. It is time to start approaching sales as an art –

the art of persuasion. By treating the prospect as a person and acknowledging the unique emotions and challenges they face, you unlock a far more collaborative approach to sales – high-ticket sales.

Not only are you directly helping prospects improve their lives dramatically, but you also get the opportunity to earn commissions that "traditional" salespeople only dream of!

Learning and embracing high-ticket sales changed my life. Before, I was working myself to the bone. I never had the time or energy to do what I enjoyed. I never was able to spend time with my kids or go on holiday. I just never had the freedom.

These days, it's a different story. I can work from the comfort of my own home and enjoy quality time with my baby son – an opportunity I had to miss out on with my older children. My career is doing better than ever as well! I've personally closed more than $30 million in high-ticket sales.

Discovering the high-ticket sales industry – a more professional approach to sales through embracing and mastering the art of persuasion – has been a game-changer. It freed me from the soul-destroying grind of the "traditional" sales industry, transformed my work-life balance, and freed me to actually enjoy living a life I enjoy with the ones I love.

Imagine that you had that kind of freedom. What would you do with it? How would it transform your life?

The key to the high-ticket industry is the art of persuasion.

Changing your life by mastering persuasion

Persuasion is utterly ingrained in our lives. The art of convincing, coaxing, and cajoling our fellow humans is a precondition for socialization. To try and persuade others is a fundamental part of the human experience. When we fail at an act of persuasion, it can lead to some of the most intense emotions we ever experience.

Imagine the unbearable pain of writing a heartfelt love letter to your teenage crush, only for her to reject you in favor of the class bully. It is no wonder persuasion has been a source of fascination among our great thinkers for millennia, dating back to our ancient predecessors.

Persuasion happens whenever we try to impact the will of another person. The philosopher Arthur Schopenhauer argued all human beings are *will* in physical form. We either have the will to perform an action, or we do not – until someone comes along to persuade us we actually do.

There is a mountain of knowledge on persuasion out there, much of it dating back centuries. In *Rhetoric,* Aristotle wrote extensively on persuasion, and explained how speakers use ethos, pathos, and logos to persuade their audiences. Ancient Confucian thinkers in China wrote about persuasion from a political and militaristic viewpoint and articulated how persuasion, "Does not depend on the content of what is uttered alone… [but also] on the person who is enunciating it."[1]

---

1   Galvany, A. (2015, November 1). *Sly Mouths and Silver Tongues: The Dynamics of Psychological Persuasion in Ancient China*. Extrême-Orient Extrême-Occident. Retrieved February 2, 2022, from https://journals.openedition.org/extremeorient/250

This ancient proclivity for persuasion persisted into the twentieth century, when the hypnotist Milton Erickson learned how to persuade his patients through their subconscious. From the ancients to the modern world, the topic of persuasion has captivated the minds of philosophers, politicians, and psychologists alike, but it's not only an ivory-tower concern. We all use different tools of persuasion every day of our lives.

A worker in desperate need of a holiday might need to sell their boss on the value of approving a potentially controversial time off request. A teenager looking to slip away for a date might offer to trade their younger sibling free time with the TV if they would do all of the chores this week.

Ultimately, persuasion is about balancing wills with desire. Whether it is for better or for worse depends entirely on how much you pay attention to both sides of the conversation.

Persuasion can be selfish when we focus entirely on our will rather than the will of the other person. This selfishness can be banal, like when you trick your colleague into paying for lunch by saying, "I've left my wallet in the office". Or, it can be downright harmful, like when a sleazy salesperson signs a well-meaning elderly client up for a service they'll never need.

On the other hand, persuasion can be selfless. Therapy is a great example of this – we focus entirely on the other person's will, with no consideration for our own, to persuade them of ways to improve their own lives. This could take the form of counseling a friend who's having trouble sticking to his diet plan, or helping a significant other gameplan how she will ask her boss for a raise.

Sales, at its best, focuses on aligning the wills of both parties. It's not totally selfish and manipulative, nor is it selfless and therapeutic. Instead, sales can create situations that are truly win-win. Successful sales happens when a young go-getter persuades the higher-ups at a big firm that she's the best fit for the job. Or when an entrepreneur convinces angel investors to back his bold start-up idea.

When sales works, these situations don't merely benefit the person doing the selling – they pay off incalculably for the ones being sold to as well.

Despite some negative publicity, sales is in fact a noble profession when it's done right. Mastering sales can transform our businesses and careers. But the art and science of sales goes much deeper than economics. Through the mastery of persuasion principles, we can not only achieve success in sales, but also improve our lives and the lives of the people around us by encouraging more win-win scenarios.

If we can learn how to tap into and use this knowledge, we can use the power of persuasion to forge a new, highly rewarding career for ourselves. It is possible to build an approach to sales which focuses on collaboration and mutual benefit through mastering the art of persuasion.

Everything we need to build a new career using effective persuasion techniques already exists, we just need to discover how to synthesize the elements properly. We don't need to reinvent the wheel – all the resources we need are out there. All the pieces necessary to build an iPhone existed long before Steve Jobs unveiled it in 2007. Henry Ford didn't need to invent anything new to sell the world his Model T; Thomas Edison didn't create the light bulb out of thin air. Success doesn't always come from invention. Sometimes, all we need is to synthesize the right elements.

What I have discovered is a method that allows the prospect to discover for themself why they need to buy. Once a prospect makes this realization, we can apply an appropriate amount of pressure to persuade them that they cannot afford to stay static, and show them how buying from us unravels a path toward comfort.

The systematic five-step process I found, rooted in human behavior, allows us to build meaningful partnerships with our prospects founded on authority. With this strong foundation, we can sell more and feel fulfilled while we do it.

What I have also discovered is an industry where using this five-step process can create a flourishing career that promises financial freedom and the freedom to work anywhere in the world with just a laptop.

Chapters 1 and 2 of this book lay out exactly what this new industry looks like. They describe what this new high-ticket industry is, as well as the how and why behind it.

Chapters 3 and 4 build on this with the research and theory behind my five-step process – Inverse Closing™. They explain what the weaknesses are behind the traditional approach to sales and explain the theory behind how someone can be led to discover reasons to buy for themselves – not just having them forced upon them by someone else.

Chapters 5 to 9 share the framework itself. They talk you through the sales conversation step by step – sharing the processes behind guiding the prospect to trust you, then have them self-diagnose their specific pain created by their situation and helping them realize what they need.

The final step in the process is committing to improving and developing your new skills. This new approach to sales isn't something that can be perfected overnight. You need to commit to mastering and constantly improving your abilities. Chapter 10 talks you through the process of both developing your skills and building a career based on this new approach to sales.

The benefits of improved sales don't stop at the bottom line. Sales mastery also means we can shorten the life cycle of each individual sale. Deals will close faster, and we will waste less time chasing leads that go nowhere. On top of that, when we're closing sales more effectively, the process of selling becomes way more fun.

Instead of having to drag the prospect with you every step of the way, you're collaborating with them to make their lives better. Not only do you get to benefit from helping and supporting others, but you also get to start on a career which lets you dictate how and when you work – all while earning respectable commissions!

Are you ready to get started?

Chapter 1

The High of High-ticket Closing

I've been so absorbed in the conversation I've barely noticed the time slipping by, but as I glance down at the clock in the corner of my screen I realize I've been chatting to Johnny for an hour.

The conversation has flowed so easily, he feels like a client I've been doing business with for years, even though the reality is that the first time I met him was about an hour ago when he answered my call.

I can't help but warm to Johnny. He is clearly passionate about his work and that passion is infectious as I listen to him. He wants to do more, I can feel it, and so can he, but he's stuck. The longer we've chatted, the clearer that's become.

But that's why he's talking to me. He booked this call in with me for a reason: he's been hunting for a solution to his problems for months before finding me and I *know* I can help him. I sense that he's starting to believe this too.

He pauses. "I'm sorry Adam, I feel as though all I'm doing is talking about my problems – you didn't call me just so I could offload on you!"

I break into a smile and take a slight pause before I answer him – partly for effect, but partly because I feel as though I'm on the edge of a drop on a rollercoaster. I can feel my heart beating faster and I have a knot in my stomach. I'm excited and nervous, but also weirdly calm. I know what's coming next.

"Actually, hearing all the challenges you're facing has been really useful. It's made me even more confident that I have a solution that's really going to help you." Johnny makes a curious noise in acknowledgement, a clear sign he is interested and wants me to go on.

I've ridden that first drop on my rollercoaster, now I'm at the peak of the second one – you know the one, where you turn a corner and there's the biggest drop and greatest adrenaline rush just seconds away.

"I called you today to talk about a membership for a passive investment mastermind that will really help give you more freedom. You'll be able to take your capital and start investing it. This will start giving you passive income and eventually mean you can replace your income and spend more time with your family. I know you'd rather be sunbathing on a beach with your family in Santorini (he told me about his dream vacation 25 minutes ago), enjoying the sunshine and your kids' first trip abroad, than constantly being on call!"

Johnny lets out a laugh. "Wouldn't we all?!"

It's time for the close. "It's a $50,000 investment for an annual membership." The words hang between us for a beat, like the moment of almost weightlessness you have as your roller coaster car is about to plummet over the edge of the drop. Time stretches out. My heart beats faster. If this were a movie, I'd be moving in slow motion right now.

I feel like I know what's coming, but I still wait for those words with baited breath.

Then, with a smile and just four words, Johnny breaks the spell. "Absolutely. Sign me up!"

Exhale

I'm over the drop and I'm elated. Time speeds up, everything around me suddenly seems brighter and more colorful, I have a huge smile on my face and Johnny does too. I've done it! We've done it.

I'm not only smiling because I know that the mastermind Johnny is signing up for will genuinely help him, but because this is my first high-ticket sale *and* I'm getting ten percent commission – $5,000 isn't a bad payday for a little over an hour's work!

I'm still riding the high of the high-ticket rollercoaster I've been on when I wander into the kitchen, my slippers barely making a sound on the tiled floor. My son looks up from his coloring and breaks into a huge grin, "Daddy, look at my dinosaur!", proudly pointing at the page in front of him.

As I cross the room to look at his drawing, the sale and $5,000 commission is momentarily forgotten. These moments I get to share with him throughout the day are priceless. "That's cool – what kind of dinosaur is that?" I ask him enthusiastically. While he's explaining all about the T-Rex on the page, my wife makes me a matcha latte.

I look up and give her a kiss as she hands me the mug. "How did the call go?" she asks. Suddenly the elation comes rushing back and I break into a huge smile.

"Amazingly – closed the sale!" She hugs me and then I feel my son tapping my arm, ready to show me more of his dinosaurs. I quickly glance at my watch, which tells me what I already know… I have time to learn more about dinosaurs before my next call, and my next $5,000 close.

This is the wonderful world of high-ticket closing.

What life do you want to lead?

What would the ideal life look like for you? Are you the kind of person who dreams about traveling the world, working a few hours each week and earning enough in those hours to support your wanderlust?

Perhaps you simply want to escape the 9–5 grind, avoid that mind-numbing daily commute and have more time and energy for your family. Maybe you want to be financially free so that you can give your family security and really enjoy life. Or do you have a vision of owning a villa somewhere hot and sunny, where you can escape for the winter, taking your work with you?

With high-ticket closing, any of these dreams is possible. Whatever you are imagining right now for your life is possible.

You can take calls when you want and have full control over your diary and availability. You can make big commission checks off just one call. You never have to cold call anyone. You can do this job from anywhere in the world as long as you have a laptop, headset and an internet connection.

I'm well aware that "financial freedom" and "autonomy" are promises made in various other industries. You've probably seen ads online for how you can "achieve financial freedom and have complete control of your life" with financial trading/drop-shipping/real estate/consultancy/coaching/affiliate marketing (take your pick!).

But here's the thing – all of those options are tough. They take time and energy. Often you fail more than once before you succeed. You need a large pot of money to get a business like this off the ground in the first place. In the first year or two, you're putting in 60–80 hour weeks whether you like it or not, just to get the ball rolling. They can be volatile – financial markets can shift in seconds; businesses can go bankrupt.

So, while it's true that you may eventually achieve financial freedom and live an autonomous life, do you really want the hard slog that comes first? I'm guessing no…

High-ticket is different

I know, I'm sure every one of those other industries also promises they're different, but with high-ticket closing, it's true. You see, there are thousands of entrepreneurial businesses with high-ticket offers that are desperate for skilled high-ticket closers to help them convert their hard-earned leads into sales.

These businesses typically form part of the "expert" industry – coaches, experts, and gurus passing on their hard-won expertise and wisdom. With the rise of the internet, they have realized that information and eLearning is fast becoming the next big thing.

However, they need to sell to prospects, they need to first persuade these prospects that they can help solve their problems. This is where high-ticket closing comes in – your role is to help address any final concerns and doubts in the way of the prospect committing to the offer that will change their life.

I can't stress enough how different this is from what you imagine a typical sales job to be. You don't have to be tied to your phone or laptop, smashing out call after call, to make big money. You can choose how many calls you have in a day. You can (and will!) make a significant commission on the sales. Once you master high-ticket closing, you will discover there are thousands of companies willing to pay you handsomely for your skills.

In fact, they'll be beating down your door to get you to take calls for them. But for me, the best part is the conversations I have every day. They don't feel like a struggle or a slog. I talk to interesting, engaging people. I walk away from each of my calls feeling energized and buzzing for the next one. And I am making great money doing so.

How do I do this? By using the skills and processes that I'm going to share with you in this book. The point is, high-ticket closing is not only an opportunity that's waiting to be seized, it's an opportunity that offers a rewarding career in every sense of the word – you'll *enjoy* your calls, you'll have *more time*, and you'll earn *more money*.

You also remove the risk associated with starting a more traditional business, because what makes high-ticket closing valuable is your skill – it's a talent that's *in* you and it's not reliant on anything external. Believe me – I've tried and failed so many businesses, looking for business *out there*, when in fact what worked in the end was unlocking the business in *me!*

Once you develop this skill set, it's something you'll have for the rest of your life.

Turning yourself into a valued asset

What sets sales apart from other fields is also what makes recognizing and acknowledging the importance of the skills and processes behind selling well: in sales, *you* are the key asset.

In any other form of business, there are many more barriers to entry. You need capital to invest and you need to understand the market you are operating in – once you have started, you are always going to be at risk of losing the assets that allow you to operate. Perhaps the stock market crashes, making your investments worthless. Perhaps a disaster wipes out the real estate which you had just spent a fortune developing.

In high-ticket closing, however, you don't need a wealth of resources to start or spend your time chasing opportunities to turn into a business. You are building and developing something within yourself for which *others* will chase *you*. The only things you need are a laptop, a headset, and an internet connection.

Once you have the skills to close high-ticket offers convincingly and understand the processes that allow you to do it, they are yours for life. No bank, disaster, unforeseen world event, or bad luck can take them away from you.

On top of this, you are not limited to just one market or enterprise. What is at the heart of high-ticket closing is not the product being sold, it is the people you are dealing with. When you understand the person on the other side of conversation well enough to close a high-level deal, you could sell anything.

All you need is the right skill set. A skill set they don't teach you in an average sales job. You need to learn the art of high-ticket closing.

Julian: Learning on the job

When starting out in any new field, you are going to have to pick up new skills as you go – you can't always guarantee that you will have adequate training provided. This was Julian's experience when he first started out in high-ticket closing. Previously, he had been working as a waiter in a fine dining restaurant; however, he had started itching for a new challenge and a serious sales job.

Luckily enough, he managed to find a role with a high-ticket company who were willing to take a chance on him and fill his diary with calls. However, Julian quickly ran into a problem. He began to realize there were vital parts of the process and techniques that he just didn't know.

Despite this, his employers were not giving him any support or training. Instead of being given actionable advice and support, he would at best be told to just, "Get better", "Make more calls" or "Don't take no for an answer".

In any other situation, this would be ridiculous! Imagine a football coach telling their team to simply "Get better" without ever explaining *how* – without brute force and blind luck, such a team would never score or win games!

He began looking for support elsewhere, but often that was little better. While he came across good traditional sales coaches, the content they produced was often too focused and specific or concentrated on putting out fires (objection handling is a classic example) rather than preventing them from lighting.

Julian recognized that he needed techniques and strategies for understanding the prospects themselves. For example, techniques helping to handle objections might not be needed in the first place if the objection could be identified and addressed from the very start!

It was at this point that he crossed my path.

For me, training these skills is my first priority – everyone I work with has to go through my program on how to lead calls more effectively first.

The difference before and after was like night and day. The moment Julian had the high-ticket closing skills he needed, he was off like a shot – in his first month alone he made $5,000!

Freedom, through high-ticket success

Promising that anyone could make millions through mastering sales would be irresponsible – if nothing else, it is a very big promise to make!

However, what I can say is that mastering the skills and processes behind selling high-ticket well makes the journey to earning six figures a year *much* easier than the alternatives. In addition to this, building a career as a self-employed high-ticket closer offers you an incredible amount of independence and autonomy.

You are able to take on as many or as few calls as you like, working for as long as you either want or need to work. You are also free to work wherever or however suits you.

You could go on vacation with your family and take a call or two in a quiet moment while your partner and children shop for souvenirs; or take an afternoon off to spend time with my kids or treat your partner to a nice meal. I cannot describe the sheer freedom and satisfaction of having completed a call and walking straight out of my hut onto a beach on the Maldives – diving straight back into my holiday.

Between the salary and the flexibility of the work, what you get is the ability to lead a comfortable and secure life. You also get the freedom of choice in how you can use or invest your time and money.

The question then becomes – "How can I get this opportunity?" Fortunately, even though only a few people have realized it, we're in the middle of a 21st century gold rush – high-ticket closers are in more demand than ever. Let me show you.

Chapter 2

The Hidden Industry

On the morning of January 24 in 1848, James W. Marshall was examining the channel that powered his sawmill's waterwheel when he noticed something strange glinting in the bottom of the riverbed. After having collected and tested a few samples, he made a discovery that single-handedly put California on the map – he'd found gold!

It wasn't the prospectors and miners who made the most money in the Gold Rush though. The people who profited most from the Gold Rush were the merchants. Half of California wanted to buy supplies and equipment for prospecting and the other half had things to sell, but no way to get them into their buyer's hands.

In the middle were the merchants and salespeople making money simply by facilitating everybody else making money. This is exactly how the world of high-ticket works.

The modern-day equivalent of this Gold Rush is in the eLearning/coaching industry. There are more people with knowledge to sell than ever before, and it's an increasingly profitable industry. But, just like in the Gold Rush, they need help to get their knowledge in front of the right people. That's where you come in as a high-ticket closer.

Knowledge means money

When I say that the eLearning/coaching industry is big business, I mean it. In 2021, this industry was worth $215 billion.[2] According to US entrepreneur Dean Graziosi, online education brings in $355 million *a day*.[3] Forbes has even predicted the industry will almost triple in size to hit $1 billion a day by 2027.[4]

Selling knowledge, especially in the age of the internet, is not only incredibly popular but also hugely profitable – the overheads are tiny, the cost of online delivery is low, you have access to a global audience and, when it's done well, this means there are big profit margins up for grabs.

The internet and modern technology has sparked this new gold rush. On the one hand, it has never been so easy to create high-value information products and services that can change lives – or so easy to deliver them to anyone, anywhere.

---

2 E-Learning Market Segmentation, Trends, Forecast to 2030. (n.d.). Straits Research. https://straitsresearch.com/report/e-learning-market

3 *The Knowledge Business Blueprint Review: How Tony and Dean Can Help You With The Knowledge Business Blueprint.* (n.d.). Blogging With Funnels. https://bloggingwithfunnels.com/the-knowledge-business-review-how-tony-and-dean-can-help-you-with-the-knowledge-business-blueprint/

4 Laker, B. (2022, October 4). *Every Leader Can Benefit From Coaching. Here's Why.* Forbes. https://www.forbes.com/sites/benjaminlaker/2022/10/04/every-leader-can-benefit-from-coaching-heres-why/?sh=78e7bf6f7e1f

On the other hand, the general public has more freedom to make their own choices about how to live their lives. We are less tied to traditional jobs or ways of working than ever before – everyone wants to find a way to break free from the 9–5 rat race.

In the middle, we can find the high-ticket industry working to connect the two sides of the equation. We've got high-value products, and a marketplace hungry to consume them.

I first started in high-ticket back in 2004. Back then, coaches and trainers such as Tony Robbins were embracing the value in selling knowledge and expertise as a product – Tony Robbins' *Unleash The Power Within* is a four-day conference that is still going strong to this day. This started with live talks in packed venues and created offshoot eLearning programs.

As others woke up to the fact that people were willing to pay to learn from someone else's expertise and wisdom if it helped them break out of the rat race – the eLearning/coaching industry exploded. Thousands of coaches and experts found niches in which people were willing to pay handsomely to learn from them.

Some leading examples of wildly successful coaches and experts with businesses worth seven or eight figures include:

- Paul McKenna[5], a behavioral scientist and hypnotist who has carved out a niche in applying his knowledge of the human mind to offer certified hypnotherapist programs to teach others how to help their clients control their phobias and cravings.

---

5 https://www.paulmckenna.com/

- Ajit Nawalkha[6], a coach specializing in helping his clients unlock their full potential. He operates through several key businesses, such as Evercoach – which offers coaching certification programs for people to become life, business, or health coaches.

- Dean Graziosi[7], entrepreneur, educator, and author with multiple *New York Times* best-selling books. Dean focuses on helping equip people with the right tools and knowledge to push out of their comfort zones, overcoming the fears and doubts holding people back from success.

However, these coaches, experts, and service providers didn't start their businesses to spend all of their time in sales – they either don't have the time to spend making sales calls or prefer to focus on the product itself. Instead, they look for specialists with the knowledge and experience to consistently close their high-ticket prospects.

As more and more high-ticket businesses find themselves getting more and more torn between sales and fulfillment, the demand for specialist and expert high-ticket closers has grown.

What is high-ticket closing exactly?

When a product is mass-produced and mass-marketed for a cheaper price, the quality often suffers. This means that scaling a low-ticket product generally means selling *more*. A small business providing a service costing $500 with tight profit margins might *require* ten successful sales to break even. When profit margins

---

6 https://coachajit.com/

7 https://www.deangraziosi.com/

are tight like this, companies are far less likely to want to dish out nice, fat commission checks to the people selling them.

This means they recruit a high volume of fairly low-skilled salespeople to work the phones, dialing call after call and playing the numbers game. KPIs like average call time, and number of outbound calls become the metrics on which you get assessed. It's a game of quantity over quality where salespeople dread the conversation and pray to strike lucky with a sale... no one wants that.

A high-ticket sale is a high-value, high-cost product or service – often with a price tag of at least $2,500 and rising all the way up to $100k. These could take the form of coaching programs, biz op, personal development, certifications, masterminds, educational products or other forms of online courses, 1-2-1 coaching, or consulting work. Because these courses leverage the knowledge of a business owner, and are mostly delivered online, they cost very little to deliver.

An example of this is the Lifestyle Investor Mastermind, which is dedicated towards helping entrepreneurs, executives, and many others unlock passive income streams through sharing specialist insights and strategies. In exchange for a $55k annual subscription, subscribers win $450k of value.

High-ticket products and services are often less resource-intensive, even though they have more value as part of the offer.

Someone very clever worked out that it's easier to sell one program at $10,000 than it is to sell ten programs at $1,000. It's pretty obvious when you stop to think about it though, because if nothing else you only need one person to successfully sell *once* to break even. Companies use this as a way to scale – by increasing the quality and investment of their offer, and by tightening their focus onto specific buyers or clients, they make their service more cost-effective.

What this means is that if high-ticket offers focus on quality over quantity they need an entirely different sales process from the traditional high-volume sales floors that most likely come to mind when you think of "selling".

Because of the high value of the offer and the intangible nature of the product, far more care and attention goes into designing a high-ticket customer journey to ensure the customers coming through the doors can see the value in these offers and how they can significantly improve their lives. Only then are they happy to pay the higher price tag to obtain the information – 99 percent of the time, offers like this cannot be bought and sold via a quick online transaction.

A website page can't sell a $10,000 course alone. In order to make a buying decision of this magnitude, these prospects need and deserve a conversation with another human being. But not just any human or run-of-the-mill salesperson. They need a skilled high-ticket closer.

So, who are high-ticket closers? I'll let you into the not-so-secret behind this approach…

Anyone can become a high-ticket closer

I really do mean *anyone*. You don't even need a background in traditional sales (although, in most cases it's an advantage!) – as long as you're willing to learn the skills you need to become a high-ticket closer, and put in the practice, you will get there. You don't even have to be a "natural" at sales. In fact, I'm certain the only thing holding you back from becoming a successful high-ticket closer is that you've never been offered the training or support you need to get there.

Let me ask you this, who comes to mind when you think of a "salesperson" in the traditional sense? I bet it's a man (often it is, even though women can be just as fantastic at sales) who has the gift of the gab, an extrovert. He's the kind of person who, you might say, could sell someone a chocolate teapot. Often these people are drawn into traditional sales because business owners see their natural charm and think that's enough to sell well. It isn't – and certainly not when it comes to high-ticket offers.

Both myself and most of my top students are in fact introverts! Being able to use charm and charisma makes up for lacking the fundamental skills to a degree, but it cannot replace them. When I run training and coaching on high-ticket closing, the focus has *nothing* to do with the person or their personality. It is remarkably process driven.

One of the most pervasive myths about traditional sales is that to be successful, you must be charismatic. Stale approaches rely on a salesperson's ability to charm and manipulate prospects into a sale.

Dave: Skill over style

I learned to dismiss the myth of charisma when I met Dave. I was consulting with a homeopathic remedy company, and they brought me in to oversee their hiring process for new salespeople. Dave was one of the first to interview for a sales associate position, and the initial impression he made was astonishing. I knew right away Dave was the most boring man I had ever met.

Dave entered the office carrying a copy of his resume. He was dressed in ill-fitting pleated khakis and a beige, rumpled sport coat.

"Hello," Dave said without inflection. Even the way he walked was boring, with his unremarkable shoulders slumped forward slightly.

He slid his resume across the table. He had zero sales experience, and had spent most of his five years post-college as a laboratory technician. Dave's lack of experience didn't particularly bother me, but it made my colleagues apprehensive. The hiring manager, Robert, was an experienced salesman with an old-school view of how sales ought to be.

"You talk to a lot of people during your typical day as a, uh… lab technician?" Robert asked.

"No," Dave responded. "I analyzed data from the samples we collected. Then I showed the numbers to the nurses and they spoke to the doctors about them," Dave droned.

"Fascinating," Robert said, "So, why exactly do you want to start a career in sales?"

"Because I know once I learn the process, I'll be your top performer," Dave said.

Robert looked at Dave, incredulous. I was surprised by Dave's display of confidence too, but I was equally intrigued.

"What makes you think that, Dave?" I asked.

"I never give up on a problem," Dave said. "Like in school, all the other kids would give up on a hard problem on a math test, but I wouldn't. In fact one time, Mr. Cromwell, he was my math teacher – "

"It's okay, we don't need to hear about that, Dave," Robert said.

"The point is," Dave said, "sales is just a problem to solve. And once I figure out how to do it, I know you'll be glad you hired me."

Dave was right – after a couple months training with me, Dave was indispensable, despite his complete lack of personality. His monthly sales climbed past Robert's. He stuck to his process and nailed almost every sale he took on. All the while, Dave remained the world's least charismatic guy.

This was never a problem for Dave because he didn't need charisma to make sales. His understanding of the techniques and processes meant that he never needed to use the weight of his personality to help his customers decide to buy.

When we abandon the charisma-as-a-requirement myth, we can understand the fundamental mindset behind succeeding in high-ticket closing: sales is not about charisma; it's our process that determines our success. high-ticket closing doesn't have to be the domain of "natural-born salespeople," and when we abandon this stereotype, we can treat sales with the respect it deserves as a profession.

I want to help you change your perception of "sales" and to realize that the world of High-ticket selling is much more accessible than you may imagine. Most people generally have a poor opinion of sales environments – they think of packed call centers, divided up by the paper-thin gray cubicle walls. They think of people cold calling dozens of prospects a day, regardless of whether they want to hear from them.

Let's be honest, we've all had those cold calls, sighed inwardly and (possibly very abruptly) told the person on the other end of the line that we're not interested, hanging up before we even hear their response. This is the exact opposite of how high-ticket closing works.

In conventional sales roles, training is often an afterthought. As I've said, there is a predominant (and mistaken) underlying belief that the key to success is charisma, not skill. This means people believe that to be a great salesperson, you need to have the "gift of the gab" first.

As a result, sales roles tend not to be growth-focused. Employers either believe that you have the "stuff" to succeed or you don't – if they don't believe in you, then they might not be willing to help you improve and develop into a better salesperson. Worst-case scenario: you might even get fired just for not having the right personality!

Not focusing on growth and skills is directly damaging perceptions of sales as a job role or a career. Those who are not recognised and trusted as having the right personality or energy are left out in the cold – they never get offered a ladder to climb or the opportunity to advance and ultimately start getting promotions and the higher value commission cheques.

This only leaves the option of soulless work in a call center, talking to an endless cycle of uninterested prospects while not making quite enough to live off comfortably. Needless to say for these people a career in sales is short lived and rather painful.

If you've tried sales before and had this kind of experience, I can tell you with absolute certainty that the world of high-ticket closing is different.

But the work you've done previously does not even *need* to be sales. There are countless other jobs which are an unrewarding daily grind.

A civil engineer based in California who I once coached complained of a similar dissatisfaction. His job required him to be in California, however his salary was mostly eaten up by rent – he was never going to afford to buy a home for his family.

On top of this, the hours he had to work were compromising his time with his family. During the week, he was out of the house first thing and by the time he got back at night, his kids would be sleeping. On the weekends, all he had the energy to do was sleep.

No matter what the job is, working a passionless 9–5 grind is never rewarding. Fortunately, high-ticket closing doesn't have to be a grind and, as I explained earlier, now is the perfect time to train as a high-ticket closer. The world is literally your oyster right now because there are so many high-ticket businesses who *need* people with this very specialist skill set.

Getting in at the ground floor

It is possible to group jobs together into three different categories based on the basic entry-level skill requirements: unskilled, semi-skilled, and skilled.

An unskilled worker might expect their salary to be around minimum wage. A semi-skilled worker could expect to earn around $30,000 to $50,000 annually. At these levels you have something that employees want, but the problem is that there are many who fit the bill. Job applications for these levels receive thousands of candidates for a single role.

If you want to be earning six figures or above, you need to find a career as a skilled worker, where employers need your skills, this is attained by an academic qualification from a top ten institute/college/university or you are skilled in a very specialized industry.

The problem is that the barrier to entry is often just as high as the reward. Being a lawyer or a doctor, for example, are specialized careers locked behind strict academic requirements and at least five figures of University fees or years of working your way up the corporate ladder.

So, how can you get a six-figure salary if you *don't* meet the set criteria – and have no desire to study for another degree and work your way up in a new industry?

The answer – join a growing industry which has a skill shortage.

Programming today, for example, is a highly competitive field, breaking in requires an extensive skill set and portfolio. Back in the '80s and '90s however, the industry was only just kicking off. All you needed to get involved was a basic understanding of coding and the willingness and enthusiasm to get involved! Those that did get involved at that early stage really did carve out a career for themselves, perhaps even became CEOs, execs, or industry leaders.

These days, high-ticket closing is that growing industry with a huge skill shortage. Now, you may be thinking, "There are tons of salespeople out there, why is there a skill shortage?" Yes, of course there are tons of sales people, the problem, however, is that traditional selling skills are inadequate for selling high-ticket.

High-ticket sales vs traditional sales - is there really a difference?

When people think of sales, the product being sold is often some form of tangible commodity. In these cases, it is far easier for the prospect to see, imagine, and understand the benefits that buying will offer them.

A used-car salesperson can let the car itself do most of the persuasion for them. They do not necessarily need to have the same ability to understand the buyer or to support them through finding the solution to their problems. As the prospect can see and touch what they are buying, it is easier for them to picture the value, and physically acquiring the item only helps this.

A prospect buying a car can easily imagine the convenience, pleasure, and freedom of having a new car while shopping. Once they have paid, they immediately get a payoff for their investment when they receive the keys to their new vehicle and drive it home.

In the more valuable high-ticket closing however, the product itself is far more intangible. A service such as coaching is not going to deliver an immediate result that the client can immediately walk away with. You can't see or touch the benefits of a top-tier training course at the checkout, or get to walk away enjoying the feel of a subscription to a mastermind in your pocket.

Instead of providing something tangible, these products more often than not allow the buyer to unlock a new opportunity to live a better life, make more money, feel more confident, etc. This means more skill is required to help the prospect truly understand how these products can help solve massive problems in their life, and paint a picture of what life looks like when they have solved this issue. This will then justify the investment.

What this means is that paying attention to, engaging with, and understanding the prospect takes on a new level of importance compared to traditional sales where a client tells you what they want and you offer it to them. If you don't deeply understand them, then you are going to struggle to get them to picture how you can help them and realize how they stand to benefit from listening to you – as I know from experience.

If you've ever worked in sales, you will likely know how it feels to face constant rejection. Sometimes, the rejection comes from a sweet old lady who says, "I'll think about it," after she listens to your entire pitch with a big smile on her face. Other times it comes from a dead-serious businesswoman who gives you an icy glare and says, "I'm not interested," before she dismisses you. In some cases, it comes from an angry old man who screams, "You're trying to rip me off!" as he storms off the used-car lot.

Whether the rejection is swift or slow, kind or cruel, it always feels the same to the salesperson – like a slap in the face.

When you move into high-ticket with the right skills, whether you've worked in sales before or not, you'll never have to worry about being slapped in the face (literally or figuratively!). In fact, it was one final slap in the face that set me on the path to developing and honing the techniques that have allowed me to excel at high-ticket closing.

Changing the script

Unfortunately, I hadn't quite figured out this new approach when I was at the rock-bottom of my sales career.

I was selling training programs at homes across the UK, and wasn't having much success. For days, I wandered through the flats of a large brick housing complex and knocked on dozens of doors. Mostly, I was ignored. A couple residents slammed their doors in my face. At the end of my first week on the job I had made a grand total of zero sales. I was desperate and fed up with the tired, scripted approach I was required to use.

Just when I was ready to head home on Friday afternoon, my manager called to ask if I had made a sale yet. Embarrassed, I had to tell him, "No."

"Get back out there, then!" he yelled at me. "If you can't make a single sale, don't bother coming in on Monday! And stick to the bloody script!"

I desperately needed this job. I had already failed out of a career in IT. If I couldn't make it as a salesman, I had no options. I couldn't afford to take my girlfriend away on holiday (again). My dream of a Soho loft was slipping away – I'd have to move back in with my parents and sleep in the racecar bed of my childhood. If I couldn't turn things around, I would be cooked like a steak and kidney pie.

I closed my eyes and took a deep breath. I muttered to myself, *I will close this sale. I will close this sale. I will close this sale.*

I looked down at my list and saw I had crossed off all but one address. My final chance at turning my luck rested on the shoulders of a nineteen-year-old dropout named Tim.

Moments later I was sitting in his living room. Tim was horizontal on his mother's couch scrolling mindlessly on his iPhone, *shirtless*. The sight of his pasty body infuriated me. I gritted my teeth. My manager's voice rang in my ears: *Stick to the script.*

I ran through the steps of the script in my head: *Build rapport with the prospect. Illustrate the features, benefits, and outcomes.* None of these tactics had worked on the hundreds of prospects I had encountered so far. I was sure they wouldn't work on Tim – but I had to try.

"Hello, Tim," I croaked, cordially.

"Alright," he responded. He didn't look up from his phone.

Cold sweat formed on my brow. I searched desperately for something I could use to build rapport with this kid. I saw a Tottenham Hotspur poster on the wall.

"So you're a Spurs fan?" I asked hopefully. He didn't respond.

There goes building rapport. What's next? I thought. *Oh, yeah, features, benefits, and outcomes.*

"Tim, I'm here to tell you about an amazing program. We have an industry recognized training center for you to train in. You can become a qualified plumber in just a year. If you complete our course, you can potentially have a £1000 per week salary, plus… Uh, plus… benefits!" I said.

Tim grunted, but made no effort to engage. He didn't care about the features, benefits, and outcomes of this program.

"Tim. Tim? Tim?! Don't you want to be successful? Don't you want to… be a plumber? Or an electrician? Don't you, Tim?"

Tim looked up at me, dead-eyed.

"Not sure."

Well, I thought to myself, *my life's over*. This sale had slipped away like all the others.

I put my head in my hands, trying not to break down and weep.

My terrible future flashed before my eyes: I'd tell my girlfriend, "Sorry, babe, we can't go away this summer." I'd show up at my parents' house and endure their looks of disappointment. I'd curl up in my racecar bed and cry myself to sleep every night for the rest of my meaningless life.

What really bothered me about Tim is I could see he desperately needed this program. He was a sad-sack with no prospects. Our product could help him turn his life around.

What I'm selling could actually help this kid! How can I get him to see he needs this program? I almost sold myself on the program I was trying to sell to Tim: for a brief moment, I thought, *maybe I should be a plumber.*

Then suddenly, a righteous fury overtook me. *No. I'm in control. I can do this. I will make this sale if it kills me!* I turned around.

To hell with the script, I thought. *I need to try something new.*

I took a deep breath. I looked Tim square in the eye – I just stopped and put aside my "selling" mind for a moment and looked at this kid, not as a potential sale, but through the eyes of a college tutor, assessing if he had the right qualities for a course like this. I realized that this wasn't a sales meeting – it was an interview. I had to invert the script. Wouldn't a college tutor be looking to match the requirements of the course to the qualities of the student?

What I said next caught Tim by surprise. "Tim, unfortunately from your answers I don't feel we can offer you a place, I don't feel confident that you would make the most of the opportunity if you were given the chance..." Minutes later, Tim and I were having a real conversation. Eventually, he even put on a button-up shirt. It was wrinkled, but it was a step in the right direction.

I didn't make that sale. However, it turned out to be a valuable learning opportunity that led me to develop a fresh inverted approach to selling. Before long, I was making more sales than anyone at the company. At first I was afraid my manager would reprimand me for going off script – but he couldn't argue with my results. "Bugger the script," he said. "Whatever you're doing works!"

Over the years, I improved my process. I delved into psychological research and found even more tactics like the ones I'd used with Tim. Since that day in Tim's flat, I've synthesized a new approach to sales. This new approach leverages effective persuasion techniques, not outdated manipulation techniques, to make sales a better experience for buyers and sellers.

Through many trials and triumphs I have seen a proper approach to high-ticket sales transforming businesses and people.

Today, major brands in the high-ticket space outsource the selling of their high-ticket offers to my high-ticket closing agency. My company is responsible for more than $40 million in increased high-ticket closing for our clients.

This is where high-ticket closers differ from traditional salespeople. We can collaborate with prospects so even when they don't end up buying we all still feel good about the encounter. We can change the paradigm so we don't have to push customers into something they don't want. We can boost our close ratio so fewer sales slip away. We just need to let go of the old approach and try something new.

The problem, if you're new to this world, is that very little training is provided by high-ticket businesses on how to sell high-ticket offers and if they do, the training will most often than not rely on outdated traditional sales techniques. I know this as I have listened to my clients' sales calls.

More often than not, high-ticket businesses will expect people to come in with the skills to sell their high value offers. These businesses don't have the time to spend hours in the training room with their high-ticket closers. In fact, many of these businesses are too small to even have an in-house sales team in the first place.

But instead of being a drawback, this provides you with an incredible opportunity. The growing demand for skilled high-ticket closers, combined with the majority of those working for businesses in high-ticket industries not having had the correct training, provides you with an opportunity to stand out from the crowd and become sought after by high-ticket business owners.

If you can demonstrate an understanding of the processes and skills required for high-ticket, you will automatically be a more valuable candidate than someone with a more "traditional" sales approach.

Traditional sales tends to take a shotgun approach. If one sales call fails, it is no issue to just call the next number in the list. However, as you are about to find out, this just won't do for businesses that operate a high-ticket model.

High-ticket calls are far more personal. And they need to be to get results. The "churn and burn" approach taken by traditional sales is too costly for businesses with high-ticket offers – as a high-ticket closer, each call you make might have cost the business anywhere between $150 to $300 in ads and lead generation.

These high-ticket businesses are spending *a lot* of money on paid ads to encourage prospects to book calls. The leads this approach generates are highly niched – these are people who want the information product the business is selling and who *already understand its value*. This means that by the time they get on a call with a high-ticket closer (you!), they are receptive to the offer and ready to buy. All you have to do is get them over the line.

This process of generating leads like this is called a "funnel" and it follows specific steps to catch ideal clients and guide them through the sales process. An example might look like this:

1. Paid, highly targeted advertising on search engines (Google Ads) or social media platforms (Facebook, Instagram, etc).

2. Opt in page, further copy hitting the Aviator's (Ideal buyer) pain points.

3. Video Sales Letter (VSL) with a call to action.

4. Sign-up for a "consultation call" (a sales call). In many cases the lead will need to fill out an application form in order to book the call.

5. Call with a high-ticket closer.

The high-ticket closer's role in this is limited only to the fifth step. In order to book a consultation call, the prospect will have to fill in an application form providing the relevant information and data required. The timings are even at your convenience – you set your own availability and the prospect chooses a time slot within that for the call.

This means that in high-ticket closing you can always be sure the client is both interested in your call and that you are not calling at a bad time.

It is important to be able to demonstrate care, attention, and finesse in each call. To have reached you, the prospect has already shown interest in the product. Your role is to provide the personal and human touch while checking that they are getting the product or service that truly benefits them. So, rather than "selling" it's a bit more like "matchmaking".

This skill set is easily learnt – by reading this book you are well on your way. However, before we can even begin to talk about the best high-ticket approach, we need to cover the traps and pitfalls hiding behind the "traditional" approach that have leaked their way into the world of high-ticket.

Chapter 3

Breaking Away From the Old Way

As we know by now, the world of high-ticket is very different to a standard run-of-the-mill sales role many of you might be familiar with. It requires a more subtle, skillful approach in order to move people to make life-altering buying decisions which can often be intangible at first.

However, if we are to develop this new skill set, we need to expel any idea of traditional sales, and the habits that come with it from our minds. One of the issues that the world of high-ticket faces today is that many of the salespeople who are selling these life-changing solutions fail to make this distinction. They are still stuck in a world of the traditional salesperson, and as a result end up leaking their traditional sales habits into this world with mediocre results.

This also poses a problem for the owners of high-ticket companies. When they need someone to sell their high value, elite level solutions, who do you think they go to? That's right, the people with "sales experience", and all the bad habits that come with it. This cycle must stop here.

Going to extremes to make a sale

Traditional sales is a vicious cycle of bad habits that go to extremes to make the old approaches work. On one end of the spectrum, we treat sales as a high-pressure, win-at-all costs game – the classic game of "Always Be Closing" (ABC). On the other end, we turn ourselves into glorified customer service representatives telling people what we think they want to hear – the Sales as Service (SaS) approach. Unfortunately, neither of these approaches creates the dynamic we need to succeed in the world of high-ticket.

Each approach solves some of the problems of bad sales (control in the high pressure situation and rapport building with Sales as Service), but they create even worse issues in the process because they carry the same underlying flaw: neither acknowledges our need for a radically different sales approach – one that bridges the divide between buyers and sellers and allows us to achieve high-ticket success. To accomplish this, though, we must first understand the two extremes.

High-ticket prospects are on guard against being manipulated – the fact that the tactics favored by these extreme stances are so common means that they will be smelt a mile off. Taking too gentle a stance however runs the opposite risk – if you don't challenge their perspectives, the prospect does not learn anything. If they leave the conversation with the same insights and mindset that they had at the start, they risk not committing to the sale.

This means that it is vital to be aware of them to prevent you from clumsily stumbling into them while having high-ticket conversations.

High-pressure sales: the cost of "Always Be Closing"

The first extreme approach salespeople rely on today is the idea of Always Be Closing (ABC). This approach takes the selfish attitude of nefarious salespeople to its limit. A high-pressure approach makes sales a battle rather than a collaboration. It focuses only on what the seller wants, and ignores the wants and needs of the buyer.

It's easy for high-pressure sales to seem cartoonishly unsubtle, but it doesn't usually look that over-the-top in everyday life. Real-life salespeople in traditional sectors rely on high-pressure tactics all the time. They might tell their prospect this offer won't be here tomorrow, or try to scare them with alarming statistics about how their competition will outperform them if they don't buy the product on offer.

It is human nature to turn up the pressure when we don't get our way. When we don't get the response we want, we tend to overcompensate aggressively and blame someone else for the poor result.

High-pressure, ABC sales make buyers uncomfortable and disengaged, and the approach perpetuates negative stereotypes about salespeople. These factors would be reason enough to avoid high-pressure sales on their own, but they're not the only flaws. High-pressure sales also ignores the wellbeing of the salesperson.

The damage to salespeople

One of the most dramatic examples of how high-pressure sales can be harmful, even for the person making the pitch, played out in the corporate offices of a multimillion-dollar tech company.

A scathing report about tech giant Yelp released in November 2020 by *Business Insider* revealed the company's rotten culture.[8] The source of the rot was a high-pressure sales culture. Yelp pressured its salespeople to make sales at all costs, even in the face of sexual harassment. The company prized closing above all else, and the only way they knew how to close was through pressure, pressure, pressure.

One Yelp employee said, "If I'm not closing, I'm treated like I mean nothing to this company and my self-worth suffers immensely." Another said, "'No means no' does not exist in our sales tactics."

For Yelp, high-pressure sales caused mental anguish for its salespeople. The pressure applied to the salespeople rotted the company culture, top-to-bottom. When pressure and adversarial dynamics are the only sanctioned ways to approach sales in a company, negativity abounds. Inevitably, salespeople end up suffering in such a negative environment, which only compounds the problem.

Negative thinking can tank our moods, and positive thinking really does make us feel better on a physiological level. When we are positive, we lead happier, healthier lives. Research suggests that positive thinking alone makes people less likely to have a heart attack than their more negative neighbors.[9]

---

8 Price, R. (2020, November 7). *Heavy drinking, sex tapes, and a pyramid scheme: Yelp insiders speak out about the company's high-pressure sales culture.* Business Insider. Retrieved March 4, 2022, from https://www.businessinsider.com/yelp-insiders-disturbing-stories-high-pressure-corporate-sales-culture-2020-11

9 Yanek, L. R., Kral, B. G., Moy, T. F., Lazo, M., Becker, L. C., & Becker, D. M. (2013, July 1). *Effect of Positive Well-Being on Incidence of Symptomatic Coronary Artery Disease.* The American Journal of Cardiology. Retrieved March 28, 2022, from https://www.ajconline.org/article/S0002-9149(13)01280-0/fulltext

High-pressure sales environments actively discourage positivity. Instead, these environments promote negativity and distress. It is not fair to salespeople to build a sales approach on a foundation that is bound to destroy them.

Thankfully, high-pressure tactics have no place in the world of your new high-ticket career.

Impact of ABC sales on buyers

ABC sales are bad for salespeople, but let's not forget about the poor buyers. A high-pressure approach represents everything buyers hate about salespeople who make crude appeals to emotions.

When a salesperson employs high-pressure tactics like "yes traps," warnings of scarcity , and other such manipulative techniques to overcome a prospect's objections, buyers feel like they're being played.

A "yes trap" would be an unsubtle attempt to lead a buyer towards saying "yes" to making a sale. The salesperson will ask questions to which the answer is clearly yes, such as, "If I could show you a car which gets great gas mileage, you would buy it today… right?" Their intention being to manipulate the buyer into feeling guilty if they were to change their answer to "no" when confronted with the choice to actually buy.

While scarcity does genuinely make products more appealing – limited-edition sneakers will have teenagers desperate to look cool in the latest trends lining up around the corner – in the hands of a salesperson, it just seems sloppy. Being told *"This program is $10K – however, if you buy it now, it's $5K; but if you come to us* *tomorrow, it will be $10K"* does not inspire confidence in buyers – it reeks of manipulative deception.

Buyers, especially those in the high-ticket world are smart, and they've had years to learn how to avoid pushy salespeople. Just as it is human nature to apply pressure when you don't get what you want, it's also human nature to recoil when pressure is inflicted on you.

Salespeople in a high-pressure approach apply pressure to buyers, which triggers the buyer's fight-or-flight response. They look for the first opportunity to leave or retaliate against the pressure we're applying. When a salesperson adopts an adversarial attitude, the buyer will be more than willing to play the hero and thwart the sale at their first opportunity. We will build on this idea of resistance in the next chapter.

ABC sales is not a sustainable model for sales, but it's an even greater problem for high-ticket. If a prospect thinks they will miss their chance to buy something, pressure will cause them to close a deal quickly. However, if the prospect feels confident they could buy somewhere else tomorrow, pressure will drive them away just as fast. The market today provides consumers with endless options, and pressure only works when the buyer thinks they don't have any other choice.

Salespeople who practice this like to focus on how many prospects they close, not how many they let slip away. But, for every sale made using a high-pressure approach, how many are lost by making prospects feel harried and annoyed? In the world of high-ticket, where every lead is precious, you cannot afford to sell like this.

In high-ticket, your reputation is absolutely vital for success. Given that you are operating in the online space and selling intangible services, your prospects will be more skeptical than usual – they will be looking out for confirmation that their instinct to not trust immediately was justified. Bad reviews thanks to a sloppy salesperson can add up to millions of dollars lost in sales.

If we want to succeed in high-ticket, we need to tap into a better process. Both buyers and sellers need to come out of each conversation feeling amazing, not like they've just finished a heavyweight fight.

This leads us to the other extreme, the sales as a service approach.

Sales as Service:
How to be a glorified customer service agent

Since most people don't want to feel like their job is hand-to-hand combat, many salespeople have tried to move away from high-pressure tactics. This has led to the rise of the "Sales as Service" approach. Although it might make buyers and sellers feel more comfortable, Sales as Service does not offer a model for success either. In some ways, it is even less effective than the high-pressure alternative, particularly in a high-ticket environment.

Unfortunately, the service end of the sales spectrum lets go of what actually works about the high-pressure approach: maintaining the salesperson's control of the process. Sales as Service cedes all the control to the buyer and turns salespeople into glorified customer service representatives.

High-ticket conversations are exploratory (as we will soon learn). They require the closer to be able to guide a prospect through the decision making process, which at times means challenging their beliefs. Constantly being a yes person agreeing to the whims of your prospects, you won't get very far.

Rather than serving only the will of the salesperson, like the high-pressure approach, Sales as Service serves only the will of the buyer. When we adopt a Sales as Service approach, we lose sight of what it means to be a high-ticket closer: we focus on serving our prospects to the detriment of our own success.

The appeal of Sales as Service is rooted in our cultural preference for stellar customer service. There isn't much that can make us like a company more than when the customer service is excellent. With so many options available to consumers, buyers will go out of their way to do business with companies that offer good customer service – even if it means spending more money.

Over time, traditional salespeople recognized this and have tried to implement this customer-centric thinking into their sales approach. We try to keep customers satisfied, even if it means wasting time and resources on prospects with no intention of buying from us.

In service-oriented sales, closing is an afterthought. When we adopt a Sales as Service approach, salespeople feel their primary goal is to be a resource to help the prospect rather than create a situation that benefits both the buyer and the seller.

Why Sales as Service can't work in high-ticket

It never hurts to offer good customer service, but a customer-service-based approach doesn't work for high-ticket. The reason is simple: to sell High-ticket, it requires the high-ticket closer to become an authoritative figure, not a passive counterpart. Such a position allows the high-ticket closer to be in control. Control is key for sales, especially in high-ticket – But not in the way the high-pressure approach tries to grab it. It is not about giving the buyer what they think they need, or even helping them choose a specific option. High-ticket sales is about providing new insights and guiding a non-buyer toward becoming a buyer.

Sales as Service is an appealing approach because we all like to be served once in a while. When salespeople adopt a Sales as Service approach, everyone involved feels better, especially when we are used to high-pressure sales environments. It's a breath of fresh air for buyers and sellers when a salesperson asks their prospect, "What can *I* do for *you*?" There is no sense of manipulation. Buyers and sellers leave a sales interaction, whether a sale happens or not, with a positive feeling.

Sales as Service in the movies

The classic Christmas movie *Miracle on 34th Street* represented the Sales as Service idea all the way back in the 1940s.

In the movie, the real-life Santa Claus convinces Macy's salespeople to send customers to a competitor so the Christmas shoppers can buy the toys they need.

"I don't get it," one of the shoppers says when Santa tells her to head over to Gimbel's. "I just don't get it!"

Of course, in the film, everyone loves this customer-first stunt. It promotes the giving spirit of Christmas, and it turns out to be good for business, too. Santa makes everyone happy with a Sales as Service approach. It's easy to see the appeal for salespeople: most of us would rather be like Santa Claus than one of the pricks from *The Wolf of Wall Street*. But Santa

Claus doesn't have to worry about quotas or commissions – if you want those nice fat commision checks from high-ticket closing, you need to think about this differently.

Because the Sales as Service approach removes pressure, the salespeople who adopt it don't make any effort to nudge their prospects toward buying. Service-oriented salespeople try to influence prospects by positioning themselves as friendly resources.

If you take this approach with a high-ticket, you are going to end up telling your boss about that "really good conversation." that led nowhere. You don't have any commission and your prospect still has a problem that needs solving, it's a lose-lose.

How Sales as Service hurts the buyer

From a buyer's perspective, the Sales as Service approach might not seem like a bad deal. *All the control, and I don't even have to buy if I don't want to? Sign me up!* Though they might not realize it, Sales as Service is actually bad for buyers too.

When we fail to lead prospects, we fail to serve prospective buyers effectively. The Sales as Service approach puts all the pressure on the buyer to decide what to buy, even if it's what they need. Buyers must navigate a complicated, ever-growing marketplace alone.

With every purchase decision they feel like they've been handed a ten-page wine list, filled with foreign words they don't recognize. With no authoritative waiter to make a recommendation, what will they end up drinking?

Buyers *think* they want salespeople to adopt a Sales as Service approach. Indeed, it is generally more pleasant than dealing with high-pressure tactics. What buyers don't realize is that Sales as Service is bad for them, because it doesn't solve their problem. It doesn't make the overwhelming tsunami of choices they face any easier to navigate.

Choice paralysis

There is a well-observed phenomenon in economics called choice paralysis. A study conducted by researchers from Stanford and Columbia in 2000 illustrates how it works. When customers in a supermarket were presented with six different jelly options, they would consider the different flavors and buy one. When customers were presented with 24 jelly options, the customers became frustrated and often bought no jelly at all.[10]

We might think we want lots of options when making a decision. However, in reality, when consumers are overwhelmed with choices, they don't know what to do. They feel the need to weigh all the options equally, but they can't. When there are too many choices the working memory can't hold onto them all to compare them.

In the unlikely event a customer does buy a jar of jelly off the wall of 24 flavors, their decision will either be based on price, or another random factor like the name of the flavor, the design of the jar, or how easy it is to reach on the shelf.

---

10 Geerts, F. (2017, August 17). *The jam experiment - how choice overloads makes consumers buy less*. Medium. Retrieved February 28, 2022, from https://medium.com/@FlorentGeerts/the-jam-experiment-how-choice-overloads-makes-consumers-buy-less-d610f8c37b9b

Our job as salespeople is to help guide our buyers through choice paralysis. The art of being a waiter in a fine dining restaurant is understanding their patrons and directing them towards the specific options that they would enjoy. Instead of presenting them with overwhelming freedom, a good waiter provides a structured framework that helps the patron move towards making the order they will most enjoy.

Sales as Service doesn't do this – it is merely the opposite of high-pressure sales. However, in this case, doing the opposite doesn't quite work. While high-pressure sales people essentially say, "Do what I want," Sales as Service reps say, "I'll do whatever you want." Neither of these approaches end in a sale that benefits the buyer and seller.

The solution for high-ticket closers is not to apply more pressure through high-pressure tactics. Nor is it to remove all pressure and treat sales as a service. It's that sweet spot somewhere in the middle we need to define, then learn to harness.

Achieving sales harmony

Humans like moderation. Philosophers dating back to ancient Greece promoted "moderation in all things." This maxim of moderation doesn't only apply to cookies, wine, or binge-watching TV. It applies to all human endeavors, including our approach to sales. The best outcomes often come from seeking the middle ground between extremes.

By comparing the two extremes of ABC sales and Sales as Service, we can learn valuable information on how best to synthesize the two approaches and arrive at a harmonious middle ground for high-ticket closing.

The main benefit of ABC sales approach is that it maintains a salesperson's sense of control in the mind of the buyer. ABC selling puts salespeople in the driver's seat and leads prospects toward purchases. It allows salespeople to take charge and navigate buyers up the treacherous mountain of options they face.

The main benefit of Sales as Service, on the other hand, is that it makes buyers and sellers feel good. Sales as Service promotes a more positive dynamic between buyers and sellers.

What if it was possible to maintain control for us as the seller and still have it feel good for the buyer?. Then we see the rough outline of our new approach to creating amazing high-ticket conversations that get results for you and for your prospect.

The middle-ground approach which we take with high-ticket is distinct from the other approaches we've touched on so far. This means that we need to put a tangible, solid definition behind our new approach.

Once we can properly define this new, happy medium we can create a wonderful conversation perfectly crafted to our high-ticket environment. With this approach, we can maintain the control we gain from high-pressure selling without losing the feel-good factor of service-focused selling for our prospects. This new approach is called Inverse Closing™.

But in order to make our new approach work, we must radically reimagine sales. We must redefine selling itself.

Chapter 4

A Better Way to Close

So, what is selling? And what is buying? When you bring both of these acts back to their most basic level you arrive at the same conclusion: they are *human behavior*. But let's take this one step further. In order to act (i.e. to actually buy something) you first have to make the *decision* to do so.

Now we're getting somewhere. But what needs to come together to enable us to make a decision? The answer is logic and emotion.

Aligning logic and emotion

When our sense of logic doesn't align with our emotions, our decision-making ends up getting paralyzed. Studies from cognitive neuroscientist Antonio Damasio and his research team illustrate how decision-making becomes impossible when logic and emotions are out of whack. As a high-ticket closer, this means when we fail to align our prospects' emotions and logic, their resistance will keep them from joining us in the sales process.

We often assume logic is the only ingredient we need to make a decision. However, logic and emotion can affect each other to a surprising degree.

Damasio's award-winning research shows that emotion is more integral to decision-making than we might think.[11] One of his most famous case studies illustrated this point through the story of a man called Elliot.

Elliot: Unemotionally indecisive

For most of his life, Elliot was an ordinary man. He had an ordinary job, ordinary hobbies, and an ordinary family. He was well-liked by his friends, neighbors, and colleagues. Then, one day Elliot awoke with a splitting headache. He went to the doctor and was rocked by the diagnosis. Elliot had a brain tumor, and it needed to be removed immediately.

Fortunately, Elliot survived the operation. Thanks to the handiwork of his surgeons, Elliot's brain was fully intact. His doctors told Elliot he could resume all his normal activities. After his intense medical scare, everyone around Elliot was relieved to see him return to his ordinary life – little did they know his problems were just beginning.

It was instantly clear to everyone who knew him before the operation that, post-op, Elliot seemed... *off*.

Before his brain surgery, Elliot was a tremendous worker and a leader at his company. After he returned to work,

---

11 Damasio, A. (2008). *Descartes' Error: Emotion, Reason and the Human Brain*. Vintage Digital.

though, he left basic tasks unfinished. His job performance tanked. Strangely, when his boss called him in to ask what the problem was, Elliot said there was no problem. He could identify all his responsibilities and explain why he performed them. The only part he couldn't explain was *why* he suddenly sucked at his job.

Elliot's life spiraled out of control. Without prompting, he was incapable of starting his day and getting himself to work. At work, it became clear that he could not be trusted with managing his own workload or schedule. His ability to make effective decisions had utterly vanished.

In this condition, he was unable to make decisions about the priority of the various tasks he might be called to do throughout the day. Instead of being able to determine the most important task at hand and deliberately choosing to do it, he would instead find himself doing whatever he found most interesting at that time.

A striking example of this would be spending entire afternoons deliberating on the best way to categorize papers. Despite being fully aware of the various logical options and their benefits, he would find himself incapable of the simple task of choosing an option and following through on it.

Eventually, he was fired.

His doctors, despite their best efforts, remained at a loss as to *why* his capacity for decision-making had suffered so much. His brain seemingly functioned normally—his cognitive function and reasoning were as strong as they ever had been. In conversations, he had the same pleasant disposition he had pre-operation. If he met a stranger, they would assume he was an ordinary man with his life together.

With nowhere left to turn, one of Elliot's doctors referred him to Antonio Damasio. Damasio had researched strange neurological cases like Elliot's before. If nothing else, Damasio would offer a fresh set of eyes to Elliot's confounding case.

At first, Damasio was perplexed about Elliot. There was no data from brain scans or other tests to indicate a problem. As a scientist, this lack of clear evidence didn't offer Damasio a firm footing to proceed with his research on Elliot's life. Despite the haziness, though, Damasio persisted. He conducted extensive interviews with Elliot to find what caused the tragic changes in his life.

Damasio was struck by Elliot's apparent ordinariness. There were no external indicators that Elliot was a man in crisis. His memory was sharp, and he recalled to Damasio with great clarity everything he endured in the years since his operation.

While Elliot's recollection of his life was accurate, Damasio noticed something strange about *how* he communicated his story—Elliot seemed detached from the sadness and despair he should have felt when recounting the worst moments of his life. In fact, Damasio noticed Elliot never indicated how he *felt* during any of his tragic retellings. When he spoke about his life, he was indifferent, as if his stories had happened to someone else.

Then, Damasio had a breakthrough. He realized that the source of Elliot's problem could not be found in the surface-level, logical, conscious mind. The answer was much deeper: it must be in the unconscious mind, where emotions dwell.

Elliot's sense of logic was still intact, but his ability to feel or notice his own emotions had vanished.

Elliot's emotional detachment provided Damasio with the answer – that Elliot was no longer able to integrate emotions into his decision-making process. He was able to rationally process information about the alternatives, but he had no sense of how he felt about them. Without the ability to notice or assign positive or negative emotions to the options available to him, Elliot was incapable of forming a preference as to what to do.

The result of this was that Elliot either was incapable of forming a decision or drifted from choice to choice without taking personal agency in what he ended up doing.

Our culture tends to promote "logical" over "emotional" decision-making, but this doesn't reflect how the human mind really works. Positive emotions guide us towards decisions that our reason and experience show us are beneficial, negative ones help us recognise the bad decisions. Without either, we have nothing pushing us to make a choice at all.

We don't like to think our base emotionality is driving our decision-making, so we often rationalize our decisions afterwards. However, the fact remains: our emotions are in the driver's seat of all our decisions.

As high-ticket closers, it is our job to help our prospects understand and process their emotions to make a decision. Through helping them realize which options in front of them are pleasurable or painful, we enable their emotional responses to help them find the logical solution to their problems.

It is important, however, that our prospects do not decide entirely on emotion alone. A purely emotional buying decision alone is ultimately a whim – the prospect might end up feeling "buyer's remorse" and regretting their decision when they have time to logically examine their choice later. That is when the dreaded refund requests can come trickling in, and that commission check you've been thinking about what to spend on evaporates before your eyes.

A successful high-ticket sales model needs to balance both logic and emotion equally by guiding the prospect through the process of aligning their reason with their emotions.

Fortunately, we don't need a Ph.D. in neuroscience to align our prospects' emotions with their sense of logic. I've already done the work of integrating the science, and I've laid out examples of this new approach throughout the rest of the book.

Buying is a decision

We can apply the knowledge that emotions and logic must be aligned as we implement our new approach to sales. To understand selling in this way, we must show our prospects that they have powerful reasons to act and powerful reasons not to be inactive, that they will experience positive emotions, and leave behind their negative emotions when they buy from us.

So, let's return now to the question I posed at the beginning of this chapter: what is selling? Based on what we've just learned, we can arrive at this definition:

> *Selling is presenting compelling reasons (logic) and evoking powerful emotions in a prospect, with the aim to make a positive buying decision.*

If buying is a decision, and to decide anything we need to align our logical side of our brain with our emotional side of our brain, then this definition seems right. But hold on a minute, I hear you cry, isn't high-ticket closing different to standard selling?

Salespeople have long had the intuition to align emotions and logic, which is why we sometimes inundate our prospects with information or use emotional manipulation techniques. Unfortunately, these tactics only create more resistance from prospects. It erodes the trust we need because these approaches don't respect our prospects' autonomy. Simply telling people why they should do X, Y or Z to avoid dissatisfaction, is not good enough for High-ticket, because that will invoke resistance.

The classic '90s comedy film, *Tommy Boy*, demonstrates a perfect example of why just imposing emotions on the prospect simply won't work.

We're burning alive!

In an iconic scene, Chris Farley's Tommy is desperately trying to make a sale to a high-powered hardware store executive, the first that day to not reject the sale immediately. Tommy is deeply emotionally invested – he needs to sell enough brake pads to preserve the auto parts company he inherited from his father. The hardware store executive however is not committing to the sale – he clearly needs more convincing.

When a technical explanation from Tommy's partner fails to land, Tommy takes the emotional angle. His progressively bizarre attempt to kindle emotions in his prospect serve as a classic example of why directly telling someone how they should feel or forcing emotions on them simply won't work.

Tommy invites himself to demonstrate the experience of his brake pads using two model cars sitting on the executive's desk. As he narrates the scene, acting it out with the cars in his hands, the executive looks increasingly concerned – these model cars are clearly valuable to him.

Tommy accelerates a car towards a heavy-looking item on the desk, stopping it dramatically a centimeter before he smashes them into each other. "SCREEECH!! Whoa… that was close" Tommy narrates, wiping his brow. The executive looks relieved that the models are still safe.

Tommy doesn't allow that relief to last. "Now! Let's see what happens with the *other* guy's brake pads!" Ignoring all attempts to stop him from the now horrified executive, Tommy grabs the other car and repeats his demonstration.

"You're driving along, Your kids are yelling, 'I've gotta go to the bathroom, daddy!' – 'Not now dammit!'" Tommy shouts – then suddenly, "Truck tire! SCREECH! I CAN'T STOP!" The executive's face falls as Tommy smashes his prized model car. Broken pieces fly everywhere.

Instead of taking the man's upset and confused expression as a cue to calm down, Tommy pours gasoline onto the smoldering wreck of his pitch as it turns out what he just smashed the model with was a lighter. He sets the tortured wreck of the toy on fire.

"And your family's screaming 'Oh my God, we're burning alive!'" Tommy bellows, flailing his arms around with the burning toy clutched in his fingers. "'I can't feel my legs!'" Tommy yells, screwing up his face and imitating the voice of a small child. Then he screams. The executive's eyes open wide with shock.

Suddenly, Tommy snaps out of his insane act, and adjusts himself back into a calm voice.

"All because you want to save a couple pennies." Tommy tries to commiserate with the executive.

Unsurprisingly, the executive responds: "Get out. Now." What had been a tentatively interested prospect at the start of the scene has now clearly decided that he wants nothing to do with this offer at all.

Although this is a wildly comical example of fear-driven emotional manipulation at work, the traditional sales landscape is rife with these techniques. As you can see, forcing people to your way of thinking, or trying to elicit an inauthentic emotional response from a prospect will not be the most effective way of making a high-ticket sale.

While emotions are something that high-ticket closing does aim to evoke, they need to be the prospect's own authentic emotions regarding their pain points and the benefits of the solution you are offering. The only authentic emotions evoked by Tommy's direct and blunt attempts to impose emotions were horror and disgust towards Tommy himself!

In his book *Pre-suasion*[12] Dr Robert Cialdini explains the issue at hand here as "What is focal is presumed causal". To put this simply, when reaching a decision or feeling an emotion, people hold what is currently the target of their attention as being responsible for their decision or what they are feeling.

In high-ticket sales, we want the prospect to be focusing on the emotions coming from their personal and unique needs and pain points. When a prospect is focusing on how accepting the solution you are offering will address their own authentic feelings around their pain points, they will credit their own realization of the offer's value for their decision.

However, when a prospect's attention is on you as you are pushing them towards making a decision or trying to directly evoke and impose emotions on them, they will hold you responsible. They will see you as a source of external pressure forcing them to decide and manipulating them. As with Tommy, they will be too distracted by you to pay attention to the solution.

Nobody likes to feel like they are being forced to feel or act in a certain way, and by attempting too hard to elicit or inflict a response like this in your prospect is a tired, dated tactic that won't do for our new, high-ticket skill set.

This idea that selling is something salespeople do *to* buyers is a pervasive myth. It's the approach salespeople have taken for decades, and it is still baked into the way many people practice sales today.

---

12 Cialdini, R. B. (2018). *Pre-suasion: A Revolutionary Way to Influence and Persuade*. Simon & Schuster Paperbacks.

The challenge, however, is that this myth is so deeply-rooted in how we perceive the concept of sales that it has even seeped into our language. Many common sales phrases imply sales is done *to* the prospect:

- *"I* pitched her my idea."

- *"I* closed that prospect."

- *"I* sold him the car."

These all reflect an implicit belief in the expected approach to sales: selling is a process inflicted on the buyer. This narrative undercuts both salespeople and prospects from the start as it leads us to believe that selling is merely a matter of convincing a prospective buyer, putting us in an adversarial relationship with them. *This is the opposite of what we do in high-ticket conversations.*

The outcome for high-ticket closing is the same – to help the person in front of you arrive at a buying decision – but it isn't quite so simple as presenting those good reasons and evoking emotions. High-ticket requires sophistication because the "products" you're selling are, by their nature, intangible. You're not selling a car, you're selling transformation. You're selling change.

All humans are preprogrammed to resist change, it can be scary for all of us. It can make us resist making a buying decision.

I know what you're thinking. When we "present" our logical reasons to buy, it means they are being told what to do – but no one likes to be told what to do. If high-ticket by its nature involves change, and this resistance towards both change and being told what to do is present from the outset – how do we overcome that hurdle?

To illustrate how to accomplish this, let's look at the fable of the Wind and the Sun. This folk story shows us how when we create the right environment for our prospects, they will happily join us on a journey toward a sale.

The Wind and the Sun: Selling a comfortable change

One day, the Sun and the North Wind see a man wearing a beautiful, stylish, and expensive coat walking down a quiet road. The North Wind decided that this man looked a little too arrogant, flaunting his fine coat. He decided he would teach this man a lesson. The North Wind proudly told the Sun "You see that man there? I bet you that I can get rid of his fine coat – I'll blow it right off!"

The Sun laughed and said "It's a bet."

The North Wind blew a massive gust of wind straight at the man. However, instead of blowing the coat away, the man started to clutch it tighter for warmth. The North Wind became frustrated – that should have worked!

So the North Wind blew again, harder and colder. Again, it didn't work. The shivering man only clutched his coat even tighter, desperate to stay warm.

The North Wind had had enough. "That coat is coming off now, if it's the last thing I do!" With one last freezing gale, the North Wind blew so hard that it knocked the man to the ground. The coat however, stayed on. The man was clutching it so tightly now, it seemed stuck to him.

The Sun could only laugh at the North Wind's failure. "It's my turn. Watch this."

With those words, the Sun began to shine brighter and hotter.

Noticing the rising temperature, the man pulled his collar away from his neck. "What strange weather we're having" he commented to himself.

Smiling wider now, the Sun continued to raise the temperature.

The man started sweating. However, he continued to stubbornly hold his coat tight around him.

The North Wind sneered at the Sun, "Look! You're doing no better!"The Sun said nothing, but blazed even brighter and warmer.

With sweat streaming down his face, the man finally realized what he needed to do. He threw off his coat and breathed a happy sigh of relief. After taking a second to enjoy the warmth on his face and his new-found comfort, he continued on his journey.

The Sun smiled in triumph, and the North Wind blustered away to bother someone else.

The parable of the Wind and the Sun shows us how, rather than attempting to force our prospects to change, we simply must provide them the right circumstances to prime them to make the change for themselves.

The Wind is essentially trying to tell the man what to do with every gust – "take off your coat!" The Sun on the other hand, is asking a question: "Don't you feel a little hot right now?" When we adopt this framing as high-ticket closers, we put ourselves in a much stronger position to guide our prospects toward making the best decision for themselves.

This parable shows us how indirect pressure can be more powerful than the strongest uses of force. The Sun raised the temperature to encourage a logical response from the man (removing his coat) and in doing so, the man experienced an emotional response to his choice (relief).

One of my favorite contemporary sales gurus is Oren Klaff. In his revolutionary book on sales, *Flip the Script*, Klaff explains how the human mind is fundamentally mistrustful of outside information – if there's a button that says "do not press," our automatic instinct is to press it. So, to persuade people to do what we want, we must make them feel like the idea comes from within *them*, not us.[13]

Therefore, in sales, we must allow the person to whom we're selling feel that buying is their own idea, just like the gentleman who decided to take off his coat in our parable above. Klaff calls this process "inception". If a prospect feels we are forcing the idea of buying onto them, they'll throw up walls of resistance and try to escape. However, if it feels like their own idea, they will happily move through the process with us. Inception – making our prospects feel that buying is *their* idea – is central to Inverse Closing™.

---

13 Klaff, O. (2019). *Flip the Script: Getting People to Think Your Idea Is Their Idea.* Portfolio.

My Inverse Closing™ approach that I'm about to share with you allows the prospect to unravel the good reasons and evoke positive emotions for themselves. By drawing their attention to what they need to see, you're creating the environment and letting them find their own way to where you want them to be.

Therefore, we must fine tune our previous definition to something that is more accurate to fit high-ticket.

> *Selling is the skillful process of directing a prospect's attention to their own compelling reasons (logic), evoking powerful emotions, with the aim of facilitating a positive buying decision.*

With high-ticket, it is never about *you*, it is all about *them*. If prospects see these good reasons coming from you and sense that their emotions are being forced, it will be perceived as your ideas, not theirs, thus invoking resistance. Whenever you can guide your prospects to imagine and think of ideas themselves, it will be perceived by them as their own and therefore will not be resisted.

It's subtle, but this is the major difference between sales and high-ticket closing. I'm going to teach you how – without using tactics from the traditional sales approaches I've already discussed – you can take the path of least resistance by getting your prospects to voice the reasons and evoke emotions for themselves to help them reach a buying decision.

Now that we understand what selling truly is for high-ticket – giving us the bases to build our new approach – we're ready to dive into Inverse Closing™. Just like an architect draws upon his blueprints before constructing a skyscraper, we can construct our new sales system based on our new understanding of what high-ticket closing is.

Five Phases of Inverse Closing™

Understanding why high-ticket sales work isn't enough by itself to do it effectively. Knowing what materials and parts make up a house doesn't mean you can just build your own without any support or guidance – you need a blueprint and guidance on what to do and when.

Over my twenty years of experience as a sales expert and coach and through having trained hundreds of high-ticket closers, I have come to realize the value of having a script and framework to follow. Particularly when starting out, it always helps to have something to follow – making sure that you can focus on the prospect without missing any important steps.

To support this, I came up with the revolutionary Inverse Closing Method™, a five-phase step model designed to enable success in high-ticket closing. My Inverse Closing Method™ has been tried and tested through over 150,000 sales calls – what that means is that I've had thousands and thousands of hours to fine-tune and hone in on exactly what works (and what doesn't).

Through making a first impression as a guide able to help, then understanding the prospect and the nature of their pain, we can better present them with the good reasons and evoke emotions they need to come to a decision all on their own. In essence, rather than us trying to do the closing, we inverse the process and have the prospect close themselves, hence Inverse Closing Method™.

The key thing that high-ticket closing is trying to achieve is having the prospect commit to a change by making a buying decision. Even if this is a change which is in their favor, it's our job to help our prospects to believe in the change itself and in their ability to benefit from it.

As for how we do it, science has the answer. Beliefs drive behavior. This means that if we want someone to naturally act in a certain way, we need to ensure they have the corresponding beliefs first. The study of behavioral economics – how people's emotional and psychological condition affects their economic choices – has discovered five beliefs that we can address to change someone's behavior.[14]

- *This Change Is Better Than Stasis – An individual's beliefs about the advantages of changing their behavior need to outweigh the disadvantages.* For our prospects, doing nothing is the easiest option and seems safest. We need to make sure they realize that maintaining their status quo will not relieve their pain. They will only see an improvement by enacting change as the result of making a buying decision.

- *This Change Will Make Me Feel Good – The individual feels anticipation that changing behavior will lead to a positive*

---

14 Wendel, S. (2020). *Designing for Behavior Change: Applying Psychology and Behavioral Economics.* O'Reilly.

emotional reaction and result. It is not enough that changing will reduce their pain now, prospects ought to feel what they're buying will actively increase their happiness. For this to happen, the prospects need to have considered and pictured how much better off they'll be once they have changed.

- *Everyone Will Love That I've Changed – An individual needs to believe that others will approve of the proposed change.* Committing to change is far easier when you know that it's a socially popular move – particularly with the people closest to you. In order to make a buying decision, a prospect needs to be confident that their partners and other significant relationships will support the change. This happens when a prospect is able to discover how their social status and relationships benefit from having changed.

- *This Change Feels Natural To Me – An individual needs to believe that the proposed change is consistent with their self-image or identity.* To fully commit to a change, it needs to be something that matches up with how the prospect sees themselves – a self-declared introvert who hates engaging with people will never naturally choose to be a life coach for example. This means that the prospect has to be confident that the change is aligned with their self-image and is something that they can picture themselves doing.

- *This Change Is Achievable – An individual needs to feel capable of changing their behavior.* It is not enough that the prospect feels that they *want* to change, they also need to believe that changing is possible. The change needs to feel within their grasp and as simple as possible to achieve. If they have unaddressed concerns and doubts or if the buying decision feels too overwhelming, they will not want to commit.

Ultimately, nobody can force someone into genuinely believing something. Each of these five beliefs needs to come from the prospect themselves through them having expressed the ideas and reached these conclusions without feeling that you are imposing them onto them. As a result, helping the prospect form these five beliefs is your top priority during the call.

If the prospect has all five beliefs by the end of the call, they will have no reason to not commit to the buying decision. On top of this, since the decision has naturally come from them, they will be excited and motivated to move onto whatever comes next.

The five phases

Instilling these beliefs is not something that can be done while you are half-distracted and robotically repeating the same script in every call. This process is far less about discussing the offer itself – a website could do that – and far more about focusing intensely on the prospect themselves and tailoring the conversation to them specifically. This is the only way you can successfully support the prospect through the personal and emotional revelations which create these beliefs in them.

Each of the five phases of the Inverse Closing Method™ are designed to support this process of guiding the prospect through making this closing decision. Each phase is designed to work with and support the next – it is important to follow each step in order. If you do so, then the prospect will naturally reach the conclusions that led to the five key beliefs almost for themselves!

Introduction:

The first step in guiding and supporting any prospect is to have their trust and for them to view you as an authority. The Introduction phase does this by helping you establish a sense of authority from the start. Having successfully achieved this, the prospect will want to work with you and trust your authority to make that change.

Investigation:

Your next job is to gather all of the raw data and facts so that you can start building a more detailed picture of your prospect and their situation. By knowing how to approach and structure this fact-finding investigation, you can lay the foundations on which you will then build by starting to instill the five key beliefs.

Interpretation:

Once you have the objective facts, it is now time to start understanding their more subjective and emotional meaning to the prospect so we can understand the pain of their status quo. Having as much of the emotional context as possible in as much specific detail as possible means we can build the beliefs that *Change Is Better Than Stasis* and *Change Will Make Me Feel Good* far more effectively.

However, for these beliefs to align with their self-image enough to be convincing, we can't make assumptions or make conclusions on the prospect's behalf. As much as we can, we need to make sure that everything is coming from the prospect, not us.

Through forming and asking carefully worded pain-evoking questions, we start helping the prospect share their own emotions and start to realize how and why their situation needs to change.

At this point, we also start laying the foundation for *Everyone Will Love That I've Changed* by also prompting them to examine their relationships. As they realize the problems they are facing, they also realize that those important to them are also suffering and will also benefit from change.

Implication:

Now you understand the facts and emotions around the prospect's situation and issues it is time to start providing them with the motivation and urgency to change. This builds on the information gathered in the Investigation and Interpretation by asking them to compare their status quo with the future they actually want.

Drawing their attention to how their current status quo disadvantages them with the negative implications helps them to realize that *Change is Better than Stasis*. Having done this, you help them to imagine a brighter future through accepting your offer with the positive implication – helping them realize *Change Will Make Me Feel Good*. In fact, not only will they feel good, but the positive impacts of the change on their relationships mean *Everyone Will Love That I've Changed*.

Having done your job right in the Interpretation is crucial here. By asking the prospect to picture the negative implications of not changing versus the positive implications of having changed, we are trying to help the prospect realize that maintaining the status quo doesn't align with their self-image while changing does. If we do not have a sufficiently detailed understanding, it will be impossible to help the prospect believe *This Change Feels Natural To Me*.

Inform:

Once the prospect has decided to change and feels that *This Change Feels Natural To Me*, it is time to offer them the opportunity to do so. The Inform phase is designed to demonstrate to the prospect that *This Change Is Achievable* by presenting them with the offer and making the opportunity to accept as smooth and painless as possible.

Using all the information you have gathered, you are able to demonstrate how the buying decision benefits them directly. Not only this, but you will have already identified and neutralized any of the potential complications that might make deciding to change harder for them.

Once you have learnt the script, the only thing left is mastering and perfecting your approach. In Chapter 10, I walk you through the script in action – showing you what an authentic Inverse Closing™ high-ticket call looks like in practice. Then, in Chapter 11, we wrap up by looking at the final step – embracing mastery.

Chapter 5

Introduction

"You never get a second chance to make a first impression."

~ Will Rogers

In his book *Pre-Suasion*, Dr. Robert Cialdini, says, "what we present first changes the way people experience what we present to them next."15 In other words, the first impression is crucial. As Will Rogers rightly said, you don't get a second chance to get it right.

If you show up to a first date wearing a pleasant perfume, it sets the tone and suggests your date is in for a nice evening. However, if you show up still sweating from a workout and in desperate need of a shower, your date might have second thoughts. (I found many parallels with selling and dating, not just the fact that it's a numbers game!) Cialdini's research illustrates that a myriad of factors influence our initial impressions, and there are numerous

---

15 Cialdini, R. B. (2018). *Pre-suasion: A Revolutionary Way to Influence and Persuade.* Simon & Schuster Paperbacks.

ways to provide the right "psychological frame" to lead people toward a desired outcome.

If we want to succeed at Inverse Closing™, a well executed Introducion is key. After the initial greeting I typically have a two minute Introduction. The objective of the Introduction phase is to frame the sales conversation in your favor to allow you to have authority in the sales conversation to then be able to lead the prospect.

If we botch the opening moments of a sales conversation, it can be almost impossible to recover. Unfortunately most of the techniques salespeople use to start a sales conversation fail to create the optimal dynamic between us and our prospects. In fact, most introductory techniques cause the sales process to end before we've had a chance to start.

Some bad sales introductions can be very high energy. These over-the-top introductions come on too strong and cause our prospects to put their guards up – an overly excitable salesperson instantly triggers the prospect to think, "OK, what is in it for you?". This makes it almost impossible for us to access the emotional information we'll need later in the sales process to turn up the heat and motivate the buyer to take action.

The other end of the poor Introduction spectrum is to surrender authority – a timid telesales representative tentatively asking their prospect, "Is this a good time to call?" When we come on too weak and make a meek first impression, the buyer fills the power vacuum and dominates the call.

When we fail to establish ourselves as the authority, we fail to establish ourselves as our prospects' guides, we lose control of the process. That's why it feels like the rug's been pulled out from under us when we lose a sale.

Many salespeople are taught to build "rapport" in the early stages of the sales interaction. This usually involved feigning interest with questions like, "Where are you located?" or asinine comments like, "Hey, my neighbor has the same dog as you!"

However, these tactics come across as phony and undermine our authority as high-ticket closers . Not only is it not necessary in high-ticket – you build rapport naturally by totally understanding them – but this overly-friendly behavior turns prospects off.

Contrary to conventional wisdom, prospects don't buy from their friends – they buy from the people they believe to be an authority. We're much better off presenting ourselves as authorities on our product than as potential friends for our prospects.

The root of the problem is a misunderstanding of what rapport building is. It's based on the view that if we, the salesperson, can be liked and can befriend the prospect then they will buy from us. But the view that the prospects will buy from you doesn't always come from being liked.

"Well, you're a crappy bowler!"

The perils of trying too hard to please people can be seen easily in pop culture. In the TV show *Parks and Recreation*, the main character, Leslie Knope, is a people pleaser. She is a master at building rapport to achieve what she wants.

At one point in the show, Leslie runs for city council. During a focus group organized by her campaign, a gruff guy says he won't vote for her because she doesn't look like someone he could go bowling with. Leslie takes this comment as a personal challenge.

Leslie organizes a bowling event for the campaign, going to great lengths to impress him and secure just one single vote. At the bowling alley, she adopts an exaggeratedly laid-back demeanor – the opposite of her usual Type-A personality. Leslie challenges her target to a friendly game, and he accepts. She feels like she's winning him over. They bond over beers, and Leslie even lets him win the game to make him feel superior.

Despite this effort, after the game she discovers that he hasn't changed his mind – he still won't vote for her. Leslie blows up at him: "Well, you're a crappy bowler! And I pretended to lose to you!"

Leslie's attempt to build rapport with her prospective voter is a spectacular failure. As mentioned earlier, rapport building defined by friendship building is a commonly espoused sales technique, but as Leslie's bowling fiasco implies, it is not always a guarantee for success.

When we are in a high-ticket conversation, it's not about friendship. *Phony* salespeople attempt to create the illusion of friendship for the duration of their sales pitch by building rapport with prospects. In Inverse Closing™, rapport building is to understand the prospect's situation better than they do and for the prospect to have a perspective of themselves that was not there before.

This way you are developing a relationship far beyond the surface level of phony friendship. In Inverse Closing™, you are getting them to open up to you about where they are, where they want to be, and how that relates to what you have to offer.

The Introduction phase's purpose is to establish that authority. When the prospect trusts your ability to help guide them towards a solution that will solve their problems, the call will be more effective.

Phase	*Objective*
Introduction	To be perceived as an authority and to take control
Investigation	
Interpretation	
Implication	
Inform	

Guiding up the mountain of sales

In Inverse Closing™, salespeople must take the authoritative role of guide for our prospects. The old saying goes, "It takes two to tango," but every dance has a leader and follower.

In sales, we are the leader. If we fail at the outset of a sales call, we cede control of the process to the prospect, and force them to act as their own guide. We fail to uphold our responsibility as the high-ticket closer. We must show the buyer their path, through the pain of their ineffective status quo, toward the logical sense and emotional pleasure of buying our solution.

Literally speaking, there isn't much that can go wrong when the path is low-stakes. What could go wrong with a gentle stroll in the countryside, or buying bread in the supermarket? When the stakes are higher however, guides become more important. A dangerous trek in the wilderness or making a $50,000 investment requires the support of someone who can guide you through the risks safely.

Of all the places on planet Earth to trek, none is higher-stakes than Mt Everest. Climbing to the highest point above sea level is so dangerous that no one in their right mind would attempt to summit the mountain without the help of someone experienced and who knows the mountain inside and out to guide them.

Of these guides, none are as authoritative as the Sherpas – climbing Everest without a Sherpa is almost impossible.

Sherpas spend their entire lives learning every inch of the mountain, and always know the best route to navigate up the treacherous path to the top. Without Sherpas to guide them, climbers wouldn't make it halfway to the summit without falling into a crevasse, being crushed by a sudden avalanche, or vomiting their guts out from severe altitude sickness.

Sherpas always know how to make the climb – and when not to climb at all.

Kami Rita Sherpa has traversed Everest a world-record 26 times.[16] No one is more authoritative on Everest than Kami. So when he announced one day he would not guide any travelers to the summit for the rest of the year, they accepted his counsel – even if his reason came from an unexpected source.[17] Kami had dreamed of the mountain.

Kami trudged through the snow near the peak, as he had so many times before. The cold was so bracing, his body was almost entirely numb. It's the kind of cold you never get used to. A couple of rich adventurers trailed behind him. They kept a slow pace, but Kami had navigated worse climbers to the peak before.

The wind howled, drowning out the sound of Kami's footsteps in the snow. Each breath required monumental effort in the thin air. With his years of climbing experience, though, Kami had formed the muscle memory that told him the exact right pace at which to move. As he turned back to check on the climbers behind him, he saw his careful, confident steps had left them far behind him.

Better slow up, Kami thought. He took a breath and looked up toward the peak.

Then, he saw her. A figure in a billowy, blue dress whose body looked like it was made of snow and ice was descending from the peak, straight toward Kami. She glided along, effortlessly – the harsh

16 Sharma, G. (2022, May 9). *Nepali scales Mt Everest for record 26th time.* Reuters. Retrieved November 24, 2022 from https://www.reuters.com/world/asia-pacific/nepali-scales-mt-everest-record-26th-time-official-2022-05-08/.

17 Sharma, G. (2021, May 25). *Record-breaking Sherpa says Mountain Goddess Warned him from 26th Everest Ascent.* Reuters. Retrieved April 15, 2022, from https://www.reuters.com/world/india/record-breaking-sherpa-says-mountain-goddess-warned-him-26th-everest-ascent-2021-05-25/

wind and snow had no effect on her. Kami knew this was some sort of spirit of the mountain.

Kami knelt down out of respect for the spirit who approached him and looked at him with the kind eyes of a mother.

"Kami," she said, "go back. Now is not the time. You must not return until I send for you."

Kami understood.

Then Kami woke up from his dream.

When Kami told his clients he couldn't take them up next week because a mountain spirit told him not to in a dream, they were confused. But who were they to question Kami? They said to each other "He's been to the top of Everest more than any human being, ever! If anyone has a personal relationship with a mountain spirit, it's this guy." If Kami believed it wasn't safe, then they would trust him.

Kami's clients' willingness to stay off the mountain reflects his ultimate authority as a guide. He is totally in control, and every move is his decision – including whether to move at all. Likewise, when we act as guides for our prospects, every decision in the sales process must reflect our expertise and inspire the same trust from our prospects.

From the very first moment of a sales call, we must establish ourselves as our prospects' guides. To accomplish this, we must first break their pre-existing expectations for how a sales interaction is supposed to go.

Humans and patterns

Humans are pattern-finding machines. These patterns help us to recognize familiar situations and respond to them more quickly and efficiently. For example, if we hear a loud noise that sounds like a gunshot, our brain will quickly recognize the pattern and activate our fight or flight response, allowing us to react quickly to potentially dangerous situations.

Similarly, our brains develop patterns for social behavior and communication, allowing us to interact with others more effectively and navigate social situations with greater ease. While pattern behavior can be useful, it can also lead to biases and assumptions based on past experiences and limited information.

If an interaction fits a certain pattern, we fall into our scripted steps automatically. A woman who wants to avoid unwanted attention might reflexively inform a man asking her for the time that she has a boyfriend before she has processed the question.

Prospects have recognized similar patterns in salespeople and developed their own scripts to avoid their tiresome tactics. When a pattern is recognized, the prospect will mentally disengage and act out their script on autopilot.

A weary prospect might cut off every salesperson they interact with and demand that they, "Just tell me how much it'll cost." Likewise, a beleaguered buyer might instinctively shake their head and tell salespeople who come to the door, "I can't today, sorry," without even listening to what we're selling.

Stale patterns cause our prospects to seek out the quickest resolution. When they feel every sales interaction is predictable, they have no reason to open up about their emotional pain. Instead, our prospects try to suss out key pieces of information as quickly as possible, without listening to our whole pitch. They just want to know how much it costs.

Prospects just want to learn the elements of the offer or its price. As soon as they have this information, they try to wrap up the call. "Let me think about it and get back to you," they say, which really means, "I already know how this ends and I'm not interested."

For our new Inverse Closing™ approach to work, we must break out from our prospects' predetermined patterns. We need them to be present, listening, and willing to trust our authority to guide them.

To do this, we must shatter their expectations. If you are not performing your side of the script that they are expecting, they will be forced to reconsider their assumptions and break away from responding reflexively.

That's exactly what I did when a pack of hooligans tried to rob me.

Pattern: interrupted

After a raucous evening at the bar celebrating a friend's birthday, I had completely lost track of the time and where I was. My warm buzz quickly turned to icy panic when I realized where I was – dressed up to the nines in a seedy part of town at 2am by myself. I was a prime target for a mugging.

Trying to push worrying headlines out of my mind, I balanced my options. I had to make it to the Underground. My options were a four-block walk through a notorious neighborhood or a 45-minute detour. In my beer-buzzed condition and against my better judgment, I found myself deciding to risk the direct route.

As I entered the neighborhood, I immediately felt I was being watched. Unfortunately, the feeling was not just my imagination. There were six teenagers staring at me from across the road. Before I could look away, I caught the eye of the only girl in the group – she stood straight and calm, surrounded by glaring burly boys who towered above.

As we locked eyes, her expression shifted from boredom to malicious glee – target locked.

Nervously, I looked down and picked up the pace. I was painfully aware of my Gucci loafers and Rolex. I started walking even faster. The station and safety were *so close*.

Unfortunately, I was only following her script. She pounced out of an alley in front of me, barely able to contain her excitement at having intercepted me.

"Have you got a light, mister?" she asked, pulling a cigarette from behind her ear. A movement in the shadows of the alley warned me what would happen next. If I followed their script, the five boys would jump me instantly.

They had clearly played out this violent pattern many times before. If I wanted to escape without becoming their next victim, I had only one choice: I had to break the pattern and regain control of the interaction.

The girl repeated herself, "A light, mister. You deaf?" Her eyes glittered with promised violence as she reminded me it was my line.

I looked her dead in the eye, and with a deliberate calm I did not feel, I answered. "I am a little old man and you're going to hurt me."

The building energy of tension and anticipation evaporated immediately – replaced by confusion. This was neither the response nor emotional reaction she had expected!

Encouraged by her sudden change, I kept turning the tables.

"You wouldn't hurt a poor little old man," I said. "What would my grandchildren do without their grandpapa?"

With a confused look on her face. It was clear she thought I was crazy. She could clearly see I was barely in my 30s!

"I must be getting home to my wife," I hunched over to make myself appear small . "I haven't been this late for dinner in 63 years. Wouldn't you like to leave me alone?"

The girl stamped her foot, frustrated that she had lost control of the situation.

"Whatever." She turned on her heel. "You're not even worth it."

For a moment I was frozen in place, unable to believe my gambit succeeded. Then I realized she could change her mind at any second, and I raced along the final block, down the stairs, into the tube station, and onto the train. As I settled into my seat, I breathed a heavy sigh of relief.

Sitting on the train, I wondered how I managed to escape my assailants. If I hadn't interrupted the girl's pattern, I might've ended up bloody on the sidewalk, with no Rolex – and maybe a broken leg or two. The hooligan girl was disoriented because I failed to act according to her plan. By interrupting her pattern, I bought myself time to escape.

I had executed a classic pattern interrupt, which I had learned from years of sales practice. This experience with the hooligan girl solidified in my mind that interrupting expected patterns can be a powerful tool. Our prospects are like that hooligan girl – they have expectations for how they think salespeople will behave based on their experience with our repetitive approaches and we as high-ticket closers must do the opposite.

How can we successfully interrupt the patterns our prospects expect out of a sales conversation?

Establish calm energy

First, our energy levels need to be different to the typical sales person. Our prospects have come to expect a certain energy from the salespeople they encounter. Whether the salesperson takes a pushy and high-pressure tack, or tries to make themself subservient and service-oriented, the prospect expects a keyed-up high energy encounter. To interrupt this pattern, we must invert this expectation.

We set ourselves up for failure when we begin every call with the same hackneyed attempt at rapport building. Since we aren't scary hooligans trying to rob them, they're not afraid of us. Instead, they usually just hang up the phone with a curt, "Sorry, not interested."

Rather than displaying all our energy, we must come across with the demeanor of a neutral assessor. Even if we're excited about the potential commission we'll get from this sale, it's important to bring our energy down to a calm neutral so we can interrupt the typical sales pattern for our prospect.

At the outset of a sales call, we can disrupt our prospects' expectations in three steps. When we implement this three-step approach to the Introduction, we can disrupt the predetermined patterns, assume our rightful role as guide, and shepherd our prospects toward buying. The first of these steps is initiating control.

Step 1 : Initiate Control

A guide must lead, and leading requires control. Kami would never tell a first-time Everest climber, "Why don't you decide how we get to the top of the mountain, I'm sure it'll work out!"

He maintains control of the route and pace the climbers take to the peak. It's his decision when to rest and when to make the final push toward the summit. Likewise, if high-ticket closers are going to act as effective guides for our prospects, we must always maintain control of the sales process.

To frame the discussion effectively, we must use these techniques with subtlety. Subtle application allows us to communicate ideas about ourselves and our product without showing all our cards. If we're too obvious when we apply the frame, our prospects will feel us dragging them through a process, instead of guiding them toward a solution.

The initial moments of the call are critical in taking charge of the interaction. Starting off every sales call with a minimum of two, preferably three, questions allows us to initiate control. The purpose of these questions is not rapport-building or idle chit chat – in fact the answers don't even matter.

The rule here is the one who asks the questions is the one who is in control. The person asking the questions is controlling the direction and pace. The person answering is following their lead. By being the first to ask questions, we establish control and show our prospect that we will be their guide.

These questions should follow this pattern:

1. So, you have shown interest in (whatever specific product you're selling)?

2. How did you hear about us?

3. What do you do for work?

Crucially, we must present our questions in the form of a natural, free-flowing conversation. If we simply run through the questions like a robot our prospects will feel uncomfortable and want to leave the call at the first opportunity.

Once we've initiated control by asking questions, and using implied-relationship words, we can move to the next part of the Introduction.

Step 2: Establish authority

The next phase of the Introduction is to position yourself as an authority on your prospect's problem. Without this sense of authority, it is impossible to maintain control throughout the sales process.

Prospective Everest climbers allow Kami Sherpa to guide them because they trust his authority on everything related to climbing the mountain. This means when he says, "We will not climb today because the mountain spirit said so," they accept his assertion without question. Likewise, we must make our prospects feel that we are authorities on the sales process.

Whatever the problem of the prospect you solve with your offer, you must give the impression that you understand this problem very well and have solved it many times. Something like *"We have helped X amount of people… those that typically come on these calls have X problem which causes X pain until we worked with them."*

This statement cements our authority because outlining the problem and pain very early on resonates with the prospect and demonstrates you already understand them and their problem. Also, using the words *"until we worked with them"* implies that they can trust you to fix it, as you have a track record of delivering results.

Step 3: Cement Authority – Status Switch

When we establish our authority after initiating control, we can confidently proceed with the next step to cement our authority. The default hierarchy of a sale is often buyer on top and salesperson on the bottom, giving all the control to the buyer. However, when we interrupt this pattern, we switch up the relationship through something I call a Status Switch.

We, the high-ticket closers, become assessors, and our prospects our assessees. You can do this by first understanding you are never selling them your offer, you are always assessing them for your offer. The fact you are assessing them means the prospect should sell themselves to you – creating the status shift.

This Status Switch reverses the script and dynamics between prospect and salesperson. A traditional salesperson following "Always Be Closing!" is always selling to their prospect. In this case, what we are following is "Always Be Assessing!" – instead of the salesperson chasing the prospect's approval, we've flipped it so that the prospect is coming to us.

Somewhere in your introduction, you must outline qualities that are needed for your prospect to be a good fit for your offer such as dedication or whether they are coachable and open minded. The need for these prerequisite qualities justifies the status shift and justifies the need for you to ask deep questions to lead them. If we can establish ourselves as being of a higher status, then we can even more effectively influence our prospects. With this influence, we can assume our roles as high-ticket closing guides.

Once we've executed the Status Switch, we can further consolidate control through implied-relationship words. These are words that suggest the relationship we want to have with our prospect and allow us to subtly build a sense of connection.

Telling our prospect we will "share" a piece of information with them piques their interest and makes them feel we have knowledge they need. Likewise, using words like, "Let's explore this today," makes our prospect feel that the sales process is an open collaboration.

These implied-relationship words serve to build trust, which is crucial for the process to work. They also present our guidance in a positive way. Rather than feeling like we're dragging them up the mountain, our prospect will feel they are a part of a shared adventure whilst we still maintain control.

Our prospects will defer to our guidance, and we will dictate the pace of our journey.

By framing the interaction in this way, we have achieved the goal of establishing our authority in the mind of the prospect. Once we've established ourselves as an authority we can now guide our prospect and initiate the next step in the process: Investigation. This is where we access the critical facts about our prospects and determine how we can begin to leverage those facts to navigate them towards sales.

Chapter 6

Investigation

"It is a capital mistake to theorize before one has data."

~ Sherlock Holmes

Sherlock Holmes is completely right – you need all the facts before you can start to draw conclusions or build theories. In the Introduction phase, you learnt to establish control over the conversation and present yourself as an authority figure to the prospect. However, all the control and authority in the world won't help high-ticket closers guide prospects if there is no context for each unique sales encounter. Before a Sherpa can guide a novice up Mt. Everest, they must know how prepared the climber is.

They also need to understand what the climber is trying to achieve on Everest in addition to what the circumstances on the mountain will be. The more factual information they have around the expedition, the more effectively they can guide the climbers up the mountain.

97

Likewise, before we can effectively guide a prospect through a high-ticket sales call, we must establish a comprehensive picture of the current situation. Without this foundation, we cannot plan the proper route for a sale to happen. We need to make sure that there are no sales blind spots that might disrupt the process we are guiding our prospects through.

Throughout the Investigation phase, we become cartographers. We draw up a detailed map before we guide our prospects toward a sale. To make our map, though, we need a thorough understanding of the environment around us. If there's a raging river two miles east of us, that better be clearly marked on our map. Likewise, if we encounter an obstacle during a call that can disrupt our sales process, we must establish what that is before we blindly try to overcome it.

To make our high-ticket map and guide our prospects along the sales journey, we must establish where they are and what's around them. Then, we can chart the path to where we want them to go and achieve sales success. If you are lost and you call upon a friend to ask for directions, before giving you directions, the first thing they will ask you is "where are you now?" We must execute an Investigation that gathers the intelligence necessary to thoroughly understand where our prospects are now.

Investigation is the process of questioning a prospect to gather the contextual details we'll need to steer through the sales process.

Phase	Objective
Introduction	To be perceived as an authority and to take control
Investigation	Discover the necessary background information and facts you need to successfully make the sale and protect it.
Interpretation	
Implication	
Inform	

Unfortunately, most salespeople fail to uncover a complete picture of their prospects. Instead, they jump too quickly into finding out their motivation, asking unhelpful or awkward questions like "What's your why?". Some even start to offer the solution (i.e. our product), before they have established the prospect's terrain.

When they fail to investigate, they undermine the control and authority they have built up during the Introduction phase. This can cause a sale to spiral out of control fast.

Even a girl scout must investigate: if she doesn't understand that her aunt is diabetic, she might try to sell her the most sugary, delicious cookies rather than the sugar-free ones. Similarly, we might try to sell a coaching certification offer and pin the sale on the fact they can work remotely, but then find out they work from home as an accountant already. An incomplete understanding could risk the entire sale!

Until I understood the importance of gathering information before jumping to interpretations, I let far too many sales slip through my fingers by accidentally falling into sales blind spots. One particularly humiliating example of this happened a few years ago, with a prospect named Bill.

Pride comes before a fall

I had recently started working with a life-coaching company. After a few years of success selling for other businesses, I was confident in my new methods. My ability to establish my authority and maintain control of sales calls got me the new job, where I was hired as a manager. During my first week, I crushed every sales record. I thought I had it all figured out.

That's when a bright-eyed young salesperson named Millie walked over to my desk. "Adam," she said, shyly, "I was wondering if I could observe one of your calls today?"

Her request boosted my already-inflated ego. "Absolutely, Millie," I smiled smugly. My tone said, *Watch and learn from the master!*

My next prospect was a surefire sale: Bill. In my first two calls with him, I made a strong initial impression. Bill seemed eager to start the program as soon as possible. So, when I dialed him up, I figured Millie would only have to sit and listen for fifteen minutes, max, before Bill and I closed the deal.

As soon as he answered the phone, Bill was enthusiastic. When I gave a brief description of the program, he said, "Tell me more, Adam!" So, happily, I did. Bill hung on every word and seemed genuinely inspired by the program's benefits.

I felt totally in control of the sale. After an hour, I thought I was ready to close.

"So, Bill," I said. "I'm just going to get you enrolled?" I smiled at Millie. She looked awed by how easy it was for me.

"Absolutely," said Bill, chomping at the bit. "Just one question first, when does it start?"

"Sure, Bill, great question," I replied breezily. "As soon as I enroll you, you will get access to the online learning and your group coaching sessions will start next week."

Unlike for the preceding hour of the call, Bill didn't respond immediately. I thought we had been disconnected.

"Are you still there, Bill?"

"Yes, I'm here," Bill replied, the enthusiasm gone from his voice. "I'm sorry Adam, it's not gonna work for me."

Millie was shocked. I tried to maintain my composure. Unfortunately, Bill's dismissal shook me.

"What – why?" I asked.

"Well," Bill sighed, "I'm traveling for work next week and I'll be pulling sixty-hour weeks for the next month. We're signing a big new client. I just won't have the time."

Millie looked slightly disappointed, slumping her shoulders. She gave me a look that said, *I guess he's not so great after all.*

My face flushed with embarrassment. I was desperate to wrest back the sale. My voice grew higher and faster.

"Oh, well, you can fit it in some of the training during this week before you travel, it's just one hour a day!"

"No," said Bill, firmly. "I'd rather do this when I get back. I just don't have the time now."

For a moment, I didn't know what to say. Millie wouldn't even look at me anymore. Bill filled in the gap in the conversation.

"Best of luck to you, Adam." He hung up.

Millie got up from her chair. "Thanks, Adam," she said quietly. "I learned a lot." She raced out of the office to escape the secondhand embarrassment.

"Sure thing," I croaked. For the rest of the day, I sat at my desk, wondering what went wrong.

On my train ride home, I realized that if only I had investigated Bill's situation more thoroughly before I tried to close, I could have avoided embarrassment. Without the requisite data, I could not tailor the sale to his specific situation.

Had I asked the simple question in the Investigation phase, "Do you have any upcoming travel plans?", it would have prepared me to position his commitment around the fact he was traveling, and then things could have been different. Even when the offer seems right up the prospect's street, prospects will subconsciously look to get out a sale and they will find anything to help them do it.

Remember humans don't like change, we avoid it at all costs and self sabotage is a way to avoid change.

Assuming I knew everything I needed to know about him left me vulnerable to a sudden obstacle. I had been focusing so much on his pleasure and interest in the course that I ran straight into the trap of forgetting to check what could stop him signing up! Before I knew it, the sale was over.

The Investigation phase is critical because we don't know what we don't know. Therefore, we must find out! Otherwise, we leave ourselves open to sales blind spots and risk losing sales. Often when salespeople fail to investigate prospects thoroughly, they think the prospect is the one to blame for not telling us what we need to know.

However, as high-ticket closers it is our job to ask the questions that will unveil this information. It's not the prospect's fault we failed to do our due diligence and ask the right questions. When we fail to investigate our prospects, we might find ourselves trying to sell cheese to a lactose-intolerant vegan.

It is our responsibility to discover data about the prospect that can enhance our chances of a sale by giving us what we need to address any obstacles. When we harness the data, we can move the prospect towards the sale and address facts about their current situation before they turn into objections.

If our training program offers the prospect a career change opportunity, we must determine beforehand how long she has been thinking about this to determine if this is merely a whim or if the prospect is serious. Similarly, if we can learn at the beginning that this career change offers her the same income as her current job, we can then prepare to focus on the other benefits the career change offers.

When we learn these important facts about the prospect beforehand, we can tailor our approach to ensure we have everything in sight to achieve the sale rather than being blindsided and losing it.

Gather intelligence

The investigatory phase of the sales process is similar to intelligence gathering in the world of espionage. If we want to complete our mission successfully, we must have accurate information about the problems we might encounter along the way. To successfully gather the intelligence we need, we must know what questions to ask to attain a comprehensive picture of our prospects' world.

Intelligence gathering questions focus on the "what" – all we need at this stage is the objective facts, rather than the prospect's emotions towards things. Therefore, the answer to every question asked during the Investigation phase should be purely factual. At this stage, we are only collecting the raw data that we will use to build our map.

This also means we don't need to go too deep with our questions during the intelligence-gathering Investigation phase. If we try to jump into "why" questions before we've established all the "whats," we might be headed down the wrong path. If at any point we find our information lacking, it's because we failed to ask the right questions.

If we try to complicate the questions at this point, we run the risk of painting an incomplete or inaccurate picture. We might overlook an important detail and end up running headfirst into a trap later on. Only once we've gathered the requisite factual information can we move toward interpreting it with "why" questions – but we'll cover that in the next chapter.

Throughout the Investigation phase, we are collecting information to aid us later on. To do this, we need to stay focused on the prospect and gather data about them and their situation. Inserting our commentary or opinions in follow-up questions runs the risk of making ourselves or our own opinions the focus of the conversation – as discussed in Chapter 4, this is to be avoided.

Phony rapport-building also undermines this process. When we digress from the Investigation to talk about our own kids, or to explain how we are also looking to buy a boat, we're distracting our prospects from the sales process. The aim is not to build a relationship with the prospect at this stage, but simply to gather facts.

When we fail to gather all the facts about our prospects during the Investigation phase, we cannot fully understand the terrain we must navigate. It's like trying to build a house with only partially complete blueprints. If we start throwing up walls speculatively, we'll have no one but ourselves to blame when the roof inevitably caves in.

Each stage needs to be completed one step at a time. The time for analyzing and interpreting the facts we are gathering will come later.

The Investigation process

During the Investigation phase, we must stay on the lookout for information that will color our understanding of our prospect. We can figure out the questions we must ask to attain this information by determining what situational facts we will need and reverse engineering the call to obtain critical information. In other words, what knowledge will be necessary for us to accomplish a sale and what knowledge is necessary in order not to lose a sale?

Some details are the same for any offer, "How long have you been thinking about doing X?" or, "Are you looking at any alternatives?" for example. Other, more situational, facts or details we may require depend on the specifics of the sale.

For example, if we're selling one-on-one therapy sessions, we must know whether they have had professional help before. Later, we must revisit this point and find out why any previous therapy didn't work so we can explain how your therapy will fill in those shortcomings.

Likewise, if we're selling a business consultant certification offer that promises the earning potential of six figures, we must determine how much they are currently earning so we can contrast the offer to their current salary in the next phase of the sale process. If they already earn six figures, we can focus on other positive outcomes like working for yourself, before banging on how their life would change with a six-figure salary.

Remember that we are establishing background knowledge, not having a full-fledged conversation. Each question during the Investigation must have a deeper meaning behind it to explore later in the process. We are not interested in superficial information for the sake of it. Rather, we want our questions to provide information that is relevant to the sale.

Questions might include:

Question	Deeper Meaning
What do you do for a living and how long have you been doing it?	Where is the money going to come from to pay for the offer? Are you completely satisfied with your career, or is it lacking somehow?
Are you married?	Are you the only one who decides whether or not to buy?
How long have you been interested in this offer/ service?	How serious are you about buying? Are you a procrastinator? What is unique about now?

These questions are not designed to uncover our prospects' motivations. Rather, we are providing a complete picture of their situation. Only once we have the full picture can we dive deeper to root out their emotional problems that will be solved through the purchase of our product.

The specific questions we ask are determined by what we're selling:

Product	What do we need to know?
Investment products	Has our prospect invested before?
Training to become a life coach	How long has our prospect been trying to make a career change?
Therapy session for anxiety	What has the prospect tried before? Is the prospect looking at other forms of help right now besides your offer?
Ghostwriting services to a budding author	Has the prospect tried to write their book themselves in the past? Have they worked with a ghostwriter before?

We must learn how to frame the questions we ask around the deeper meanings we must uncover to understand our prospects.

When we ask the right investigation questions, we gain a full understanding of our prospects. The factual picture of the prospect we're selling to helps us formulate how best to proceed on the sales journey.

The Investigation process allows us to make an effective map to determine how we guide our prospects forward. To help you craft these questions you must think of two things:

- What do I need to know about the prospect that will help me find leverage to get a sale?

- What do I need to know about the prospect that can potentially lose me a sale that I can preempt and overcome later?

Once we have a complete picture of our prospects' situations, we can dive deeper into their problems. We move next from the "what" of our prospects' situations to the "why." It's time to uncover how we can motivate them to buy.

With a complete sense of where our prospects are coming from, we can question them further to learn how they arrived at their current situation that causes concerns and dissatisfaction. Then, we can determine how we can help them out of their status quo by solving their problems through sales.

Chapter 7

Interpretation

*"If I had an hour to solve a problem, I'd spend fifty-five
minutes thinking about the problem and five minutes
thinking about solutions."*

~ Albert Einstein

Whether Einstein is the one who actually said this is unclear, but the
wisdom in this sentiment remains powerful. As we work through
the Interpretation, it's important to remember to take the time
to deeply think about our prospects' problems. In fact, this is the
part of the call that is going to take up the most amount of time
and requires the most amount of skill and time in a high-ticket
conversation, so pay attention.

The Interpretation phase builds on the Investigation phase
by taking the data from the investigation as landmarks in the
prospect's terrain for us to explore. During the interpretation phase
we draw out how those elements are causing friction amounting
to voids, discomfort and dissatisfaction in their life. Ultimately we

want to build a big enough case that presents in the mind of the prospect that the status quo is unsustainable.

We build this case by creating and testing hypotheses and theories about *why* the prospect's status quo no longer works for them – establishing what their pain points are. What we need to be careful of is making blind assumptions – something that sales gurus teach us to never do. However, the trap is not making assumptions. It is jumping to a conclusion based on an assumption you never tested or verified.

Making an assumption is the first step in starting the lines of inquiry that the Interpretation phase depends on. Once we have made a hypothesis about our prospect's problem, we test it by asking questions. If the theory is confirmed, we dig deeper. If it is disproven, we look for a different line of inquiry.

With every proven hypothesis, we turn up the "emotional heat" – bringing us closer to letting our prospects close themselves. Eventually, this emotional heat lights a fire under them that motivates them to move forward.

This means that the Interpretation phase is about imitating the Sun from the story of the Sun and North Wind in Chapter 4. It is about having a conversation that helps you to discover the negative meaning and pain behind the facts you established in the Investigation phase – while simultaneously drawing our prospect's attention to them.

Unfortunately, our prospects haven't all prepared slide decks on all their emotional pain points. It's up to us as high-ticket closers to uncover these pain points ourselves. We need to build and test our theories regarding how the facts we have already uncovered cause pain, then test our ideas by asking well-crafted questions and listening actively and attentively.

Phase	Objective
Introduction	To be perceived as an authority and to take control
Investigation	Discover the necessary background information and facts you need to successfully make the sale and protect it.
Interpretation	Put the information you have discovered about the prospect into context – what are their problems and where are their pain points?
Implication	
Inform	

Often, salespeople jump on "buying signals," that flare up when a prospect shows interest in buying. These signals might look like a young car-buyer who says, "What a sick ride!" when they walk on the lot, or an eager business owner who says, "That sounds incredible!" after we tell them a particularly helpful feature of our product.

It's natural to want to capitalize on our prospects' excitement, but when we jump on these buying signals, we end up turning the prospect off. Rather than lurching after buying signals, to maintain our authority, we must stick to the process.

Selling isn't telling

Establishing our prospect's emotional pain points is a vital step in Inverse Closing™. It helps us present our prospects with the right circumstances to make them feel that buying is *their own idea.*

As we discussed in Chapter 4, humans are resistant to being told what to do and prefer to maintain the status quo if they can. This means that as high-ticket closers, we can't just tell our prospects their pain points let alone that they must buy our product.

"No one fights like Gaston"

Telling people what they want instead of listening to them is a tale as old as time – this style of pushy sales tactic is something even a child could recognise.

At the beginning of the Disney classic *Beauty and The Beast,* the villainous Gaston, a strapping and widely admired man from a small village, prepares for his wedding. Everything is prepared and ready, there's only one more task to check off the list – propose to the bride, Belle.

He is certain that, of course, she'll say yes – after all, every villager wants a guy like Gaston.

Even when describing the wonderful life he and Belle would have together, he never stops to ask what Belle actually wants. Gaston is not listening. He's selling what he *thinks* she wants rather than finding out whether he's even on the right track.

> Belle, being provided with no alternative, ushers him out the door claiming that she doesn't deserve him. When Gaston continues to ignore Belle and goes in for a kiss, he gets a door slammed in his face and knocked face-first into the mud – publicly embarrassing him in front of the whole town.
>
> Turns out, she wasn't that into him.

Gaston's approach shows us even if you can give your prospect the moon, you're still assuming they *want* the moon. Gaston's sales approach is selfish. He doesn't even pretend to care what Belle wants. Allowing our prospects to speak about their pain points in their own way shows that we genuinely care about the prospect and their situation.

This involves helping them recognize their own reasons why their current situation requires them to change. In order to do this successfully, we can't tell them their problems – they need to express their own issues and concerns about their status quo for themselves.

Let the problem speak for itself

When we frame our questions right, we can assess why our prospects are in a distressing situation and how we can help them get out of it. Many salespeople fall into the trap of jumping to conclusions about the prospect's problem instead of truly listening to them.

Closing requires the prospect to feel that the buying decision makes natural sense to them, rather than something that was pushed on them. As a result, it's much more effective when we allow our prospect to vocalize their problem for themselves, rather than telling them what we think is going wrong.

As human beings we love our own ideas, but we resist when someone else imposes an idea on us. We especially hate it if we feel someone else is telling us what our problems are. It's never a pleasant feeling!

Think about it: what would you prefer if you were learning something new for the first time and struggling? Someone to barge in, tell you what you were doing wrong, and take over? Or to have the space to work it out and ask for the help you actually want and need?

Nobody likes someone coming into their lives and dictating what their problems are. Even if you're right, your prospect will probably feel hurt and have their ego bruised if you confront them with their problems. It feels like a stranger is judging them and making assumptions about things they know nothing about. As a result, they put up their defenses and stop listening.

In a sense, the Interpretation phase is like a religious confession. When churchgoers sit in the confessional booth and lay out their sins to a priest, it's usually a relief. With the weight lifted off their conscience, they are ready for a solution. So when the priest tells them to say ten Hail Marys, they'll do it happily. It would be downright strange if, when they sat down for the confession, the priest said, "Let me guess – adultery? Yeah, I know it's adultery, you cheeky bugger!"

This is essentially what traditional salespeople do when they try to diagnose our prospects' problems instead of allowing the prospect to tell them what's wrong. What they should be doing is asking questions and actively listening to the answer. Giving your prospect the space and security to reflect on and confess their issues is far more productive.

I learnt this the hard way while selling a trading coaching program which taught how to trade options for those wanting to escape the daily grind of work. I found myself on a sales call with an older gentleman called Chris. Chris worked as a truck driver at a mining site working a job that anyone would describe as punishing. He would work 160 hours in two weeks, starting his work day at 4:30am.

The work was rewarding – he was being paid $150k a year – but it was demanding too. He expressed a concern that he was getting older and the job was taking a toll on his health. He wanted a way to maintain that income and wanted to do something more meaningful with his life by becoming a chaplain.

Here is where I made my mistake. I had connected the dots: as he got older, he was starting to feel like his age was holding him back. This was how I would create urgency in his mind to change his situation, his lack of time was of the essence! I then jumped ahead in the script and asked, "Do you feel that your younger work colleagues handle the job easier?" I instantly realized my mistake when he fired right back with "No! I can outrun any of those guys without breaking a sweat!".

I might have been right, but I really should have been more tactful. I was too forward and too direct, I had accidentally challenged his ego and put him on the defensive.

What I needed to have done was be a little more patient and been a bit less blunt with my question. Instead, I should have asked around the problem using subtlety and helped him admit it for himself – for example, "Chris, you've mentioned your age; in what ways, if any, do you think it might impact your ability to continue performing this job effectively?"

The lesson here is not to describe their situation in a language they have not used themselves and not to jump too far ahead!

This approach also helps save embarrassment and damaging your authority if you're wrong. Giving the prospect the space to speak for themselves means you can quietly test your theories about their emotional pain points without jumping to conclusions or making blind assumptions.

Pain-evoking questions

The transition between the Investigation and Interpretation phases tends to feel natural, since they're both driven by questions – the questions of the Interpretation following on naturally from the answers discovered in the Investigation. The purposes of both phrases however are dramatically different.

Whereas the Investigation is a fact-focused conversation focused on the raw objective data, the Interpretation is a pain-centric one about the prospect's emotions. In order to close, the prospect needs to believe that *Change is Better than Stasis*. This means that we need to have a full emotional picture about how their situation is currently causing them pain – and we need them to be the ones to say it!

This means that superficial questions like, "Why did you schedule this call today?" or, "What attracted you to our program?" won't do the job. These questions fail to cut to the heart of the matter because they don't provide any indication of our prospects' emotional pain points.

What we need to be asking are what I call "Pain-evoking questions". These are always framed in a negative sense where the answer is one that outlines what is negative about the prospect's situation. What we need to hear are deep responses that shine a light on their voids, discomforts, issues, and concerns.

There are two steps to forming a Pain-evoking question.

First, think of the problems and pains that the offer you are selling can resolve. A Pain-evoking question needs to be designed in order to encourage the prospect to identify these problems and pains in their lives and share them with you out loud.

Second, you need to make sure that their focus is on their negative pains here and now. The time to talk about the future and the benefits of the offer will come later. First, we need to understand – and have them express – the emotions which will help them realize that their status quo needs to change.

Maintaining a pain-centric conversation like this takes skill. A prospect might naturally gravitate towards talking about potential positive future outcomes. However, what they need to be recognizing and acknowledging is how the *absence* of those positive outcomes in the present is causing pain *now*.

Instead of asking…	Ask…
What will this new process offer you?	What is *lacking* for you *right now* in your *existing* process?
If you were to earn six figures, what would that allow you to do?	If you were to earn six figures, what would that allow you to do that you are *not* able to do *now*?
If you were able to work from home and have that flexibility what would that mean to you?	What *bothers* you *the most* about not being able to work from home and have that flexibility?

Of course, you are not going to help the prospect share everything they need to with just one Pain-evoking question. We are going to need to dig deeper and build on the answers we get in order to make sure that our understanding is more than just surface level.

The way to do this is using a common technique in neuro-linguistic programming called "chunking down" that allows us to move from the general to the specific. The more specifics in as much granular detail as possible that we can gain on our prospects' emotional pain, the better the understanding we unlock of how we can solve their problem.

In practice, asking Pain-evoking questions might look like this:

We are offering a hypnosis weight-loss program which provides a way to lose weight that does not rely on willpower and eliminates cravings. In the Investigation phase, we have found out that the prospect had already tried other diets which had not helped. Our goal is to have the prospect recognise that these other diets had not worked because they required the prospect to rely on pure willpower in order to stick with the strict diets.

Closer: "So, what is lacking for you right now with your current diet?"

Prospect: "I'm just really unhappy with it!"

(Now, this a great start – but it's not nearly enough information to work with yet. We need to dig much deeper and get as many specifics as to why the prospect is unhappy before we can move on. Imagine if we jumped straight to pushing benefits that are utterly unrelated to *why* they were unhappy – we'd lose them instantly.)

Closer: "You mentioned you have tried other diets before? Which ones were they again?"

Prospect: "Yes, [X and Y diets]"

(This moves the subject back to previous diets, demonstrates that you have been actively listening to the prospect, and is an easy way to help them start opening up with more details.)

Closer: "What is making you look at something else?"

Prospect: "I found it hard to stick to their diet plans"

(This is useful information. We now know their major issue, but we can still go deeper and turn up the heat further. Why was it hard? What were the emotions?)

Closer: "Oh? What made it hard for you?"

Prospect: "It just felt too rigid and restrictive. I always struggled with cravings – it seemed impossible to resist wanting to eat something I shouldn't."

(The prospect has now described what their problem with the other diets was – now it's time to get a bit more information on their pain and feelings.)

Closer: "Where does that leave you then? What bothers you the most about these strict diets?"

Prospect: "Well, I feel really helpless. It leaves me in a situation where I'm stuck with this weight. Either I am constantly fighting to ignore a craving and feel low or I am feeling guilty because I ate something I shouldn't. In the end, it gets so stressful that I stop trying and find myself back where I started."

(If we had directly confronted the prospect about their struggles about sticking to a diet, we might have put them on the defensive – automatically closing off at the idea of revealing their emotional pain. Asking gentle Pain-evoking questions on the other hand is less intimidating. As a result, prospects will be more willing to reveal the "meaning" behind their situations.)

It's not just the prospect who will be suffering as a result of the issues that face them. The people around them and important to them will also be affected. This means that your Pain-inoculating questions shouldn't just focus on the prospect alone. A particularly valuable relationship to focus on is their partners and families – the ones who are going to be being affected the most.

Closer: "What does your partner think of your situation? Have they been able to help you with your diet at all?"

Prospect: "Well, I know they're worried about me. They support me with eating more healthily – they've joined me on every diet I've tried. The problem is when I end up failing, there's not really much that they can do. I'm sure they'd be so happy if I was able to eat healthily and be happy with my diet…"

(With this, our prospect shows us another pain point – that their partner is also suffering as a result of the prospect's pain points. This provides another reason why their status quo needs to change – it's hurting those around them. It also helps them start realizing that *Everybody Will Love That I've Changed*, since successfully changing will help relieve the pain of the people around them.)

Pain-evoking questions open up a conversation with the prospect and avoids shutting down the dialogue or making prospects feel judged. It helps our prospects to reconsider their situation through fresh eyes. Once they have been given the time and space to consider the discomfort of their situations, we can more easily guide them towards the solution of a sale – which we shall do in later phases of the process.

Another benefit of this approach is that it is a naturally flowing conversation. Building on what they said and asking questions that react to the prospect creates rapport and shows that you are actively listening to them. This shows you're focusing on them specifically, rather than mechanically following a pre-determined script.

This helps the prospect to relax and creates the space and opportunity to reveal their own emotional issues and concerns. Armed with this information, we can start guiding them towards realizing *Change is Better Than Stasis* while also laying the foundation for the first half of the next phase.

But before we move onto the next phase, we must cover our bases and make sure we have everything in place and we have left no blind spots which might trip us up and lose the sale. This is where we bring in the Objection Inoculation™.

Objection Inoculation™

For a prospect to believe that they are capable of change, what you are offering them needs to be the most obvious and straightforward solution to their problems. If they have any objections, concerns, or doubts, they are not going to have the confidence to make a buying decision by the end of the call.

Often sales gurus will talk about "objection handling", but these objections are not something you can wait for them to bring up for you. By the time they've mentioned it, it's almost too late. The thought and its connected emotions of doubt and concern are now in their head, you're going to have to work twice as hard to manage them.

In this case, prevention is far more effective than a cure! During the Investigation and Interpretation, you might come across various reasons the prospect might want to object to the offer. The final part of the Interpretation is what I call Objection InoculationTM – guiding the prospect through the process of overcoming their objections before they have even properly formed.

As with everything up until now, the key is making sure that the realization comes *from* the client and happens on their own terms. You want to be asking questions that help the prospect discover that potential barriers can be overcome and that what you are offering is what can help them best.

Objections can be split into two categories: reasons why they can't accept your offer, and their alternative methods for solving their issues. The exact approach for inoculating against these objections depends on which category it falls into.

Obstacles to closing

For every prospect there are various obstacles or barriers that might get in the way of accepting your offer. These obstacles could be external complications or self-imposed issues or limitations that our prospect has put in their own way.

The issue is that prospects often treat their obstacles as immutable. They won't feel motivated to change because the fact they perceive a barrier makes it impossible to believe *This Change Is Achievable*. As a result, it becomes a bit of a self-fulfilling prophecy. Their emotional response to discovering the obstacle is in fact what makes it difficult to overcome.

Therefore, we need to uncover their obstacles first. Then, in order to inoculate them against the negative beliefs and emotions they need to avoid, we must ask them questions to overcome them. We must take what they view as mountains and reduce them to molehills.

What an obstacle might be will depend on the prospect and their specific situation – this is one of the reasons why making sure you understand them as well as possible is so important. However, I do find that some obstacles come up enough that they are worth looking out for.

One of the most common is a lack of some resource that the prospect needs (or feels they'll need). This might be anything from time to money or anything in between! Inoculating against a concern like this is straightforward – help the prospect either realize that not having the money or the time isn't an issue or work out a strategy to work with what they already have.

Other types of objections that often come up are the prospect's relationships – most commonly their partner or other half. If you are following my advice, you might see your prospects inoculating themselves against this! We have already seen this at work when discussing Pain-evoking questions. By describing how their partner is worried and only wants them to find a diet that works, our prospect provided a powerful inoculation against any reasons their partner might object.

As the prospect realizes why changing is important and how changing will transform their lives, encourage them to consider how *Change Is Better Than Stasis* doesn't just apply to them but also their relationships and those close to them. Once they realize that *Everybody Will Love That I've Changed*, they will start thinking of reasons why the people around them might want them to commit, rather than reasons they wouldn't.

Alternatives to your offer

Once the prospect has acknowledged their problems and decided to change, there is one other thing to be careful of. It is entirely possible that they might find an alternative way of addressing their issues. They might say, "Thanks for showing me I really need to do this but I've decided to go with someone else". Ugh!

What is in our favor here is that the prospect already approached us. What we need to know is what didn't work about their previous attempts to solve their problems and why they haven't tried a different alternative already. Understanding this can give an insight into what is causing their inaction and what they value – or dislike – in their ideal solution.

In the case of our prospect looking for help managing their cravings and improving their diet, we have already started inoculating against the alternatives already!

In the investigation, we found out that they have already tried several diets and are looking at other options at the moment when we asked, "Are you looking at other solutions right now besides mine?" Thanks to our Pain-evoking questions earlier in the interpretation, we know the other diets did not work because they were too restrictive and did nothing to manage their cravings. That the prospect expressed that themselves means that they will be less inclined to consider another "traditional" diet to be a solution.

Asking, "Why haven't you gone with…?" and "What did you dislike about…?" invites the prospect to think of and share their own reasons why possible alternatives might not be the best solutions to their problems. As a result, they become more receptive to our offer, as they can see where it meets their needs where the alternatives fall short of the mark.

Having discovered this information also supports the Inform phase later, as it helps us discover the specific aspects of the offer we should emphasize when presenting the offer. This helps reinforce *This Change Is Achievable* as we can demonstrate the direct ways that our offer fully meets all of their issues in ways that no other option can.

When we ask the right questions, we show our prospects the stakes of staying where they are. We show them their current situations are untenable, and they need solutions.

The principles of a strong Interpretation illuminate the best path forward for our prospects, not with any solution but yours. Opening them up to talk about their specific emotional pain enables us to guide them along a personalized route. By tailoring the sale to the specific emotional pain our prospects face, we maintain the personal dynamic we've built with them. With the right questions, we can continue on the path of discovering the discomfort we will remedy through a sale.

Before the Interpretation phase, all we had was a map of facts. After we've thoroughly interpreted why our prospects are in their current unviable situations, we have an accurately-plotted pathway we can follow to guide them toward a sale. By the end of the Interpretation phase, our prospects have confessed their problems and we've shown them the pain of the status quo. Now, they will be primed for the next phase.

When we perform a thorough Interpretation through well-crafted questions and active listening that help us to understand their pain and the prospect to realize their status quo has to change, we clarify our prospects' emotionally problematic situations and inspire motivation to change them. A successful Interpretation will have prospects practically begging to move to the next phase: the Implication. We are now ready to turn up the heat.

By the way, if you need some additional help in getting the interpretation of your sales call right, I've got an incredible free resource for you.

It's called the **Inverse Closing Quadrant™** and it's a complete guide on how to cover all the bases of everything you need to NOT lose the sale. All you need to do is scan the QR code below to get it!

Scan me!

Chapter 8

Implication

"Nobody ever did, or ever will, escape the consequences of his choices."

~ Alfred A. Montapert

As the quote rightly says – everything has consequences and we can't avoid the consequences of what we do (for better or worse) catching up with us. The consequence our prospects should be worrying about is the consequence of ignoring an opportunity to easily resolve an issue or pain by accepting our offer. Helping them realize that making the right choice in time means they actually *can* dodge an unpleasant consequence this time is our next job.

The Introduction and Interpretation phases give high-ticket closers useful information about our prospect's most pressing problems. To give us the best chance of making a sale, we must act on this information properly. We are much more likely to close deals when we unveil to our prospects why it's essential they solve their problems through sales.

Phase	Objective
Introduction	To be perceived as an authority and to take control
Investigation	Discover the necessary background information and facts you need to successfully make the sale and protect it.
Interpretation	Put the information you have discovered about the prospect into context – what are their problems and where are their pain points?
Implication	Shift the pain from untenable to unbearable, creating urgency for change.
Inform	

Every problem implies pain. Financial issues provoke emotional pain like frustration and anxiety. Relationship issues cause heartache and longing. Physical problems, like chronic aches, are painful physically and emotionally. If salespeople can highlight how a prospect's pain will worsen without our solution, we can warm them up to our offer. The crux of Inverse Closing™ is exploring a problem's *implication.*

Thanks to the Interpretation phase, you know what their problem is and you understand their pain points and the emotions around it. The issue is that their problems are familiar to them and they might feel like they are managing them well right now. Accepting your offer however is asking them to step out of their "comfortable" status quo and take a leap of faith on the problem changing.

I know from experience that humans are remarkably stubborn – even when they're looking for help. People would much prefer to suffer and be unhappy as long as it is familiar, because with familiarity comes comfort. We need to help our prospects realize *Change Is Better Than Stasis* and *Change Will Make Me Feel Good.* The way we do this is by challenging how comfortable their status quo really is and introducing some urgency into their need for change.

In their mind, the risk of stagnation must exceed the cost of change. Unless they realize that maintaining their status quo is far worse than risking change, they'll have no reason to want to commit today.

For example, we are selling a hypnotherapy training certification to a prospect who works as a massage therapist. We have discovered that they're in their late 50s and the physicality of their job is taking a toll on their health – countless hours of working their hands so hard has left them with pain in their joints.

During the Implication step, we'll reflect their pain points back at them, and project the pain into the future. We need to help them realize that even though they are managing the issue now, the pain that their job is causing them will only get worse if they don't change soon.

If their pain gets worse, they won't be able to provide the same quality of service. Offering worse service means they won't be able to earn the same income, which means they can't support their lifestyle any longer and so on… Their focus can't be entirely on if things are survivable and if they are managing right now. They should be more concerned about their future, not just seeing the problem and pain confined to today.

Like the parable of the Wind and the Sun, the Implication step mirrors how the Sun "turns up the temperature" so the man feels he must change his attire or else he'll pass out in a sweaty heap. That didn't happen the moment the man started feeling warm though. At first, the discomfort was annoying, but it was manageable. It wasn't until he properly realized that holding onto his coat had future negative implications that he felt any urgency to change his status quo and actually take his jacket off!

This is what we're doing in this phase. We need to help the prospect realize the negative implications to their current status quo. To do this, we bring their attention to the fact that their status quo is untenable – if they don't act soon, it will be unbearable and feel terrible. Changing on the other hand will feel amazing to them. Once they realize this, they get the deep and emotionally-driven desire to change that is the final nudge towards a closed sale.

Unfortunately, many closers fail to perform an effective Implication phase because they lack the requisite store of intel from the Investigation, or they rush through the Interpretation phase and miss the rawest emotional pain. The Implication is impossible without these preceding steps, so we must make sure we've executed them to their fullest before moving to the Implication.

Remember: the power of your Implication is proportional to the weight of your Interpretation. You can't properly persuade someone that they need to make urgent changes if you don't properly understand their situation and their emotions regarding their problems.

Rushing through the Investigation and Interpretation or not giving each detail the attention it deserves risks blind assumptions or a superficial understanding of the prospect. Without a deeper, well-tested understanding of the prospect, the sale falls apart.

A closer who hyper-focuses on surface-level issues simply can't guide the prospect through the revelations the prospect needs to believe in changing.

No matter how a high-ticket closer frames it, an Implication based on a surface-level problem demands a surface-level response. Prospects respond to the negative with, "I'll manage." What is needed is a personal and emotionally-urgent reason why, "I'll manage" or, "I'll survive" isn't how to overcome their challenges.

When our Implications fail to land, it's like misjudging our prospects: we lose two points in their minds. If we fail to tie the Implication to our prospect's emotional pain, they will think we don't understand their situation.

Our prospects will assume we're reading from a script and not listening to the present issues. It breaks the sense of trust we've built in the preceding steps, and worse, it undermines our authority. If we can't demonstrate understanding of prospects' problems, they won't trust us to guide them toward where they should be.

A complete Implication phase works in two parts: first the negative, then the positive. Balancing the Yin and Yang of negative and positive is how we show our prospects the only way to break out of their discomfort is to escape their status quo.

When we learn to balance these two oppositional forces, we can prime our prospects for the final push and summit the mountain of sales success.

The negative side of Implication

During the Implication phase, salespeople using the Inverse Closing Method™ focus on a prospect's negative circumstances. This forms a strong sense in the prospect's mind that if they fail to change, they won't be happy – in fact, the pain they're feeling now will only grow.

Focusing on the negative helps prospects see how the pain of their status quo outweighs the risk of change. Ultimately, high-ticket closers allow prospects to decide they need a change, and make them want to buy from us to make that change happen.

Therefore, prospects must feel more uncomfortable with their current situation than they do with the potential risks of making a purchase. During the negative side of the Implication process, we allow our prospects to see the stakes of inaction – that is, how bad life will become if they don't buy now.

So, if our prospect, looking for support with dating, is frustrated by attracting uncommitted partners and longing for a child, "How much more time can you afford to lose??" Likewise, if our prospect interested in investment is exhausted due to working 60 hours a week with an hour and half commute to work, "How much longer can you keep doing this?"

It's smart to tailor our questions to the emotional pain points we uncovered during the Interpretation phase by analyzing our prospects' issues, concerns, voids, and fears.

With the detailed sense of our prospects' pains, we've built up in the preceding phases, and we can make sure our Implication questions reinforce a sense of discomfort with the status quo.

The Implication phase provides the context to create urgency to provoke action from prospects. This is when a high-ticket closer makes a prospect recognise their current context feels unstable so they will want to move toward a more comfortable alternative.

One of the challenges we face here is the human tendency to dismiss pain. Our prospects have been making do with the status quo for some time now, telling themselves it's not a big deal.

People go to great lengths to suppress their negative feelings. For instance, you might have an annoying brother-in-law, but if you thought about how much his crassness got under your skin all the time, you'd be in a constant state of irritation. So you tamp down these frustrations to endure your daily life. However, any time you encounter your brother-in-law at a family gathering, those negative feelings come rushing to the forefront.

People often realize they should make a change, but feel compelled to stick with the status quo, creating an internal conflict called cognitive dissonance. This phenomenon occurs when a person holds two contradicting beliefs, creating a sense of discomfort.

To resolve this irritation, people might perform mental gymnastics to align their dissonant thoughts. For example, if a woman wants to buy a new house, but doesn't want to go through the process of packing, traveling, and unloading all her possessions, she might conjure justifications for staying in the old one. She will overlook the sinking foundation, the yappy dog two doors down, and the nosy neighbor scrutinizing her from the porch across the street.

When a real estate agent brings these agitating details to light, the prospective homebuyer's cognitive dissonance becomes harder to ignore. Rather than suppressing the pain, she might resolve her dissonance by admitting a change in living situation is the best course of action.

It's unlikely any of us stack up all our pain points and consider their total weight on a regular basis. When we do, the magnitude of our pain can be shocking. This shock, though, is what we need to motivate our prospects toward action. To make prospects feel the full weight of the pain they'll endure from sticking to the status quo, High-ticket closers must take the time to build up the stakes.

Think of this process like placing rocks in our prospect's backpack. Each rock represents a negative factor about their current circumstances. Putting one rock in the pack doesn't make much impact, but if a salesperson continues to add stones until the bag overflows, the backpack-bearer cannot ignore the weight any longer. They'd do anything to lighten the load.

The Implication phase of the Inverse Closing Method™ disables our prospects' ability to detach themselves from their problems. It's our duty to help them realize all the weight adds up to a serious burden. So, it is critical to perform an Implication phase that collects prospects' problems and piles them all into the same backpack. Once the buyer is buckling from the weight, we can nudge them to consider the possibility of an unencumbered future.

The Implication phase is not complicated – we simply ask their prospects what consequences might arise if they continue with their status quo. Even if prospects feel they are managing fine today, we can encourage prospects to imagine how the problem might grow into a terrible future. This process creates considerable tension for prospects, which we can resolve by guiding them toward a sale. Essentially what we are creating here is a fear of missing out on something or "FOMO".

The concept of using FOMO in sales is popular – however I think it is usually applied in a subpar way. You get sales gurus using it as a ABC tactic as a "fast action discount" which offers a reduced price if the prospect makes the decision immediately. Their goal is to create a sense of urgency, but focusing purely on price is far too superficial and blatantly manipulative.

A skilled high-ticket closer understands that FOMO is about far more than losing out on some discount or sale. Instead, the high-ticket approach should be to help the prospect realize something far more profound and personal – they have a genuine risk of missing out on the opportunity for a better life if they don't act.

Rather than focusing on something as mundane and short term as a discount or saving, a skilled closer asks the prospect to confront the risk of missing out on something life-changing. The way to do this is to draw the prospect's attention to their current situation – helping them realize the price of inaction by sharing the negative Implication.

A successful Negative Implication has two essential components:

1. The summary of all the main pain points from the Interpretation phase.

2. The consequential question that helps them realize how urgently things need to change.

It might look like this: a high-ticket closer for a coaching certification company has gone through the Introduction, Investigation and Interpretation phases with a prospect to build a foundation of emotional context. Then, when the prospect has the pain of the status quo at the forefront of their mind...

Closer: "Well Jane, you mentioned that you are not fulfilled and you have lost the motivation to work because you're not being challenged and are constantly feeling frustrated by the lack of challenge with no career progression. You're stuck with a salary that doesn't provide the earning you want, which seems to really affect your lifestyle. If we fast forward into the future and things stay as they are, how will it impact things?"

Prospect: "Well, my frustration will grow to the point where I just won't be able to give the service I should be giving, I will suffer financially, and if I continue down this financial road I won't be able to pay my mortgage and could lose my home. It's all very depressing to be honest."

This exchange neatly does two things:

- The summary of Jane's pain points reminds her of everything she wants to change and how her status quo is not sustainable for her

- The consequential question makes Jane consider for herself the cost of inaction

To make prospects' problems seem more expansive, we can follow up on our Implication questions to further increase the heat. However, we want to make sure we don't *tell* them how bad it is. That's why we maintain the questioning dynamic throughout the Implication phase. Remember, we want our prospects to feel like the decision to change originated from within, not that we presented it to them.

When done right, the prospect will be picturing these negative consequences and start realizing that the results don't line up with their self-image or what they want for themselves. This provides the urgency for them to change, as suddenly the prospect discovers their status quo isn't nearly as comfortable as they thought.

Providing a foundation of unease will prime our prospects to act as they realize *Change Is Better Than Stasis*. However, if we only focus on the negative, prospects can disengage. We don't want them to think, "Life is so bad, why bother doing anything about it?" So, we provide a lifeline. We use positivity for the first time in our process. We tell our prospects to take off their winter coats and put on their sunglasses, because the future looks bright and change feels better than the familiar pains they've learnt to live with.

The positive side of implication

After we establish the dire stakes of inaction, we can provide relief for our prospects by speaking to the positive side of the Implication phase. This is where we show them how the future could be so much better. Once we provide a glimpse into a world in which their emotional weight is lifted, we can help our prospects overcome their fear of change.

After we stack up the negatives, our prospects need a glimmer of hope – a promise of relief. They're ready for a presentation of how wonderful the future can be if they buy what we're selling.

We can illustrate how the future will be bright for our prospects by retracing our steps through the negative Implications we emphasized and rephrasing them in a positive way. This allows our prospects to reconsider the negative framing we've established. Once they feel the challenges presented by their negative circumstances can be overcome, our prospects will feel a sense of optimism.

Similarly, the Positive Implication also has two parts:

1. A summary of the potential positives they'll gain by making an urgent change.

2. A consequential question to help them realize how much they stand to gain by changing their status quo.

Finding the potential positives is as simple as taking the polar opposite of the pain points you summarized in the negative implication. "I'm worried about my financial stability" becomes "You have a regular and consistent income that you never have to worry about again!" Similarly, "I'm tired of always being stuck in one place" might become, "You can have the freedom to travel wherever you want, whenever you want!"

The magic words to use here are, "Imagine now". We want the prospect to be doing the heavy lifting here. Asking them to picture these positives makes it far easier for them to start realizing the answer to the consequential question before you've even asked it!

So, our high-ticket closer for a coaching certification company from earlier could ask…

Closer: "Jane, imagine now you are a certified life coach? You find yourself with a purposeful, meaningful career helping people create transformations in their lives, every day being different and bringing new opportunities to grow and develop; where now you can have financial freedom and the freedom to work for yourself from anywhere in the world, while making a real difference in people's lives. How would your life change?"

This nicely allows the prospect to imagine how the future could be brighter. Before you even ask, "How would your life change?" Jane has started imagining a better life for herself. Images of what this better career would be like are running through her head – all the more powerful because they're coming directly from Jane herself! As Jane is picturing this, she is realizing how much this better life lines up exactly with her ideal self-image allowing her to discover *This Change Feels Natural To Me.*

However, we must be certain we have uncovered the requisite information and investigated it properly before we move to positive implications.

We would make a fool of ourselves if we told a prospect, "Imagine how life would be when you can afford the finer things in life. Upgrading your car to the sports car you have always wanted will be sure to get the ladies' attention!" when the prospect wants the sports car to go on romantic drives along the Amalfi coast… with his wife.

High-ticket closing is not about pushing a product – as we mentioned before – it's about changing behavior. We can transition from the negative to the positive by focusing on our prospects' behavior. This transition point emphasizes how changing behavior can lead to a brighter future – hammering home not only that *Change Will Make Me Feel Good,* but also that *Everybody Will Love That I Have Changed* once the prospect starts enjoying the benefits!

How We Will Solve Their Problem

In the Implication phase, we make the final push toward action. When we perform this step effectively, our sales practically close themselves – since the logic and emotions that we present all originate from the prospect, their self-image and their own self-identity, they can't help but feel like *This Change Feels Natural To Me*. A methodical, negative framing followed by a swift punch of positivity readies our prospects to take the final steps toward buying.

By the end of this phase in our Inverse Closing Method™, we've primed our prospect to close on a sale. We've established a relationship with our prospect. We've gathered personal information and interpreted the data to design a personalized approach to our sale.

We've provided positive and negative Implications to encourage a prospect to enact change. We're finally ready to guide our prospect to sign on the dotted line. In the final step of the process, we can finally do what we have been dying to do all along: talk about what makes our offer great.

Chapter 9

Inform

"If the challenge exists, so must the solution."

~ Rona Mlnarik

Up until now, our main focus has been understanding the prospect and their issues. However, as Rona Mlnarik rightly says, there is a solution for every challenge. The prospect's solution is the entire reason they have approached you in the first place after all – you're the one with the answer they've been looking for.

We are ready for the last step of my Inverse Closing Method™. Now, it's time to move the conversation toward a sale. We can now harness the momentum of the previous phases and bring it to its natural conclusion, like a sled gently gliding down a snowy hill and coming to a pleasant stop outside our delightful chalet. This is the Inform phase.

Phase	Objective
Introduction	To be perceived as an authority and to take control
Investigation	Discover the necessary background information and facts you need to successfully make the sale and protect it.
Interpretation	Put the information you have discovered about the prospect into context – what are their problems and where are their pain points?
Implication	Shift the pain from untenable to unbearable, creating urgency for change.
Inform	Present the prospect with the solution to their pain which you are trying to sell.

When we accomplish the preceding steps in my Inverse Closing Method™, we give ourselves a golden opportunity to sit back and tell the prospect, "I've got a good understanding of where you are, what you're trying to achieve and how it relates to [your offer]."

With all the emotional turmoil the prospect has endured so far, it can be a tremendous relief to learn our product will solve her problem and heal her pain. In this final stage, we're not selling a simple product, service, or policy. We're providing a much-needed glass of ice water on a hot summer day.

This is where the knowledge we've gathered about our product comes into play. By this point, our prospect is already motivated to buy, but closing a deal without providing any information about our product would make us dishonest salespeople.

We must deliver the relevant information about our product to guide prospects over the final hurdle between deal and no deal. When we deliver the right, relevant information, it perfectly wraps around the prospect's mind, and the solution takes the shape of their problem. All they must do now is insert the puzzle piece. The sale is within sight.

However! Before we proceed, heed this piece of folk wisdom I learned from one of my American friends: don't spike the ball at the one yard line. If you're not a football fan, this means don't celebrate before you've closed the deal. If we slip at this point in the process, the sale may disintegrate in our hands.

The Inform stage is delicate and it's an easy place to stumble. We may be the shortest distance from the top, but we also have the farthest to fall. Every piece of the sale is magnified in this final phase. It's the last minute of stoppage time, the bottom of the ninth inning, the end of the fourth quarter. If we make a mistake now, we won't have time to recover. So, it is critical we maintain our focus and seal the deal without a misstep.

The key point to remember is that we need the prospect to believe *This Change Is Achievable*. This means that the offer needs to be presented as the solution to the prospect's issues as well being just within their grasp – the only thing they need to worry about is saying "yes".

Through Objection Inoculation™, we have already started doing this by removing possible ways that the prospect might complicate the buying decision preemptively. The only thing left is to make sure we don't mess things up and make things overcomplicated or stressful ourselves.

We do this by making sure that every piece of information we share now is tailored specifically to each individual prospect to whom we're selling. This is also the reason why it is vital to do each phase in order. Not only have they helped instill the necessary beliefs for the prospect to commit to changing, but they also will have given you everything you need to know about how to tailor the Inform phase specifically to *this* prospect.

Avoid extinguishing their interest with negative language

The primary way to foul up a sale at the last minute is by casting a dark cloud over its final moments. Failing to effectively communicate information about the product can be as detrimental to a salesperson as any other deterrent, like cost, pressure, or a misdiagnosis of a prospect's interests. Nothing makes a sale fall flat faster than a dark twist at the end.

The easiest way to lose a prospect with a communication error is by using words with negative connotations. If we use words that make our prospects wince, they might not maintain their focus on the sale. For example, if we say the word "finance," as in "let's talk about how you're going to finance this program," we prompt prospects to think about the pain they'll face from spending money.

Words emphasizing any loss in the deal (like money) can cause our prospects to consider more emotional pain, not the light at the end of the tunnel.

When we use words emphasizing cost – whether it's in terms of money, time, or effort – our prospects are taken out of the moment. They are begging for an emotional payoff, but instead they are saddled with more hardship. Therefore, we must avoid framing product information in terms of how much prospects will have to lose or spend.

Other than "cost", another word to avoid is "work." Telling our prospect how buying our product or service will require "work" doesn't inspire a sense of emotional relief. It denotes more hassle. If you say, "This program will require six weeks of work", prospects are more likely to come up with an excuse not to buy in. They probably have a job, and don't want to think of taking on another. Similarly, using the word "learn" simply smacks of school.

Another form of negativity to avoid is putting any competitors down or talking negatively about the competition in general. As high-ticket closers, we should be focusing on our product's solution. If we bring up negative information about rival companies instead, we can come across as petty, short-sighted, or self-interested, undermining our credibility.

When we bring up a competitor in a negative way, the prospect considers the rival company instead of being present in the sales process.

Imagine walking into an Apple Store to buy a new iPhone, and the person behind the Genius Bar won't stop talking about how terrible the new Samsung phone is. It would feel odd to hear your vendor complain about a competitor when you've already chosen them over everyone else.

If you execute your Investigation properly, you would already know before this point that the prospect was looking at other offers to yours. If you executed your Interpretation phase effectively, you would have had them unravel why they didnt go with them – getting the prospect to talk themselves out of the option as a result! At this stage, there is no point in undoing your work by bringing up the competition.

We can also create negativity during the Inform phase by failing to communicate clearly with prospects. High-ticket closers can confuse, distract, or dissuade prospects by presenting irrelevant product information. Information unrelated to a prospect's emotional context will only hurt the sale and we cannot afford to do this in the world of high-ticket.

In high-ticket closing, any distraction could cause our prospect to doubt our authority, and if they doubt us, the trust we've built erodes. However, if we know the right words and how to deploy them succinctly, we can maintain the cooperative dynamic we've built and serve as a guide without issue.

Proper communication is essential throughout the process of Inverse Closing™, but it is pivotal in this final phase. If we don't take care to convey critical, relevant, information with absolute clarity, we risk losing the sale. Like an airplane pilot, we must maintain our focus to guide our passengers safely down to the runway at the final moment.

Fire up their enthusiasm with positive language

When we present information, we want prospects to focus on all the positive groundwork we've laid over the previous phase of our sales process. We want them daydreaming about their new life. Our prospects still need to dot the i's and cross the t's, but by this step in the sales process, they're almost ready to celebrate their new purchase – they know *This Change Feels Natural To Me* and they are excited about how *Change Will Make Me Feel Good.*

One tried-and-true method to keep prospects feeling positive in this final step is to stick to language that evokes positive feelings. Avoiding words with negative connotations and placing emphasis on positive words lets us move prospects away from the feelings of uncertainty we raised during the Implication phase.

Rather than focusing on "cost," we can frame the purchase as an "investment." This guides a prospect to imagine the benefits they will experience and focus less on their finances. When we focus on investment rather than cost, we flip the negative thinking we've prompted and turn it into positive visualization.

While "cost" makes us think about spending and losing, the word "investment" evokes active financial strategy, cunning business knowledge, and long-term rewards.

Similarly, instead of using words like "work" and "learn", we can use "discover" to create a sense of excitement and exploration. For example, instead of saying, "You'll learn how to improve your public speaking skills," we can say, "You'll discover the secrets to captivating your audience and delivering powerful presentations."

Future pacing

Another way to build positivity is with language that builds momentum and a sense of keeping the process moving like, "As you go through the program..." This type of language keeps the sale in the present tense: for the prospect, it's happening now. It creates the sense of motion in a prospects' mind – action is happening, if they hold on for the ride, their problem will be solved any second now.

For example we can say, "There are three stages of the program, when you naturally and easily pass the first stage, you will be promoted to the second…".

Focusing on how easy it will be for our prospect to accomplish the program we're selling prompts them to shift to a positive mindset. It keeps them focused on moving forward towards their brighter futures and *away* from their untenable status quo.

We can then keep this momentum going by providing information that fills in the details of our prospect's vision for "how" they attain their new-and-improved future. This is known in sales as future pacing, and it's where we provide prospects with an easily digestible sense of what exactly they will experience from the point that they have already bought.

We use statements like "As you go through your program you will notice X…", or, "After completing your first module you'll be speaking to your coach…".

To understand these statements, the prospect must imagine themselves having already purchased the program. This technique helps the prospect to mentally experience the benefits of the program as if they have already acquired it. By doing so, they are more likely to feel emotionally invested in the product and be more inclined to make a purchase.

Another way I future pace in calls is when referring to the program, I deliberately use the word "your" instead of "the". This possessive language plants the idea that the offer already belongs to the prospect. It's the conversational equivalent of handing someone a product to help them start imagining what it might feel like to own it.

This is a technique I learned from the skilled salespeople of Istanbul's Grand Bazaar. As you wander through the bustling markets, the salesmen will often physically place their wares into your hands, creating a sense of ownership that makes it harder to say no. Once you are actually holding it, your brain labels it as "yours" and you become more likely to want to keep it.

This same effect can be achieved through future pacing and the use of possessive language. By encouraging our prospects to envision a positive future with our product and allowing them to take ownership of the idea, we are essentially placing the product in their mental hands. The decision to buy is often made before the prospect even realizes it, because they already feel a sense of ownership and connection to the product.

The final stage of my Inverse Closing Method™ is a balancing act: tone down the negative, ramp up the positive, and make sure the information provided to the prospect is relevant to their unique situation. With so many caveats to keep in mind, it's easy for salespeople to overcorrect, compensate, and reduce themselves to a rambling mess no better than the ones who read directly from a pamphlet.

How can we avoid making a critical mistake in these final moments? That brings us to the Inform phase's Golden Rule:

Keep it simple

In the Inform phase, salespeople must keep communication simple and directed toward the end goal. For example, one of the worst things we can do at the finish line is present our prospects with an array of details about your high-ticket offer.

The human mind can only process a limited amount of information. Research suggests people can only keep about four pieces of information within their short-term memory at a time.[18]

This means that each new fact, figure, or option we introduce as we are moving toward closing exponentially increases the chance we will blow the sale. Our prospects will become distracted and disengaged if we disrupt their thought-process at this critical stage. Having provided so much for the prospect to think about makes the buying decision feel far more complex and overwhelming, preventing them from feeling *This Change Is Achievable.*

Therefore, we must break down our information into small, digestible bites to keep our prospects on track.

We point them in one direction by narrowing our focus on the essential pieces of information to satisfy our prospects' need for an emotional payoff. You have already identified what their pain is in the previous phases – all the prospect needs to know is how their desires will be met and the clear solution you are offering will solve their problems.

When salespeople overcomplicate the Inform phase, prospects stop seeing a solution and imagine a breadth of new problems instead. The last thing we want at this point in the process is to raise new issues. Instead, if we focus on the same issues we stacked up in the previous phases, prospects will follow the natural connection between their problem and our solution.

---

18 Cowan N. The Magical Number 4 in *Short-Term Memory: A Reconsideration of Mental Storage Capacity.* Behav Brain Sci. 2001 Feb;24(1):87-114; discussion 114-85. doi: 10.1017/s0140525x01003922. PMID: 11515286.

Failing at the finish line

Recently, I observed a salesperson on a call with a prospect who wanted to enroll in a life coach training program. The salesperson nailed every step up to this point, and the prospect was primed to commit to a sale. She accepted she could no longer live with the purposelessness of her real estate career. She hung onto every sentence of the positive implication.

But when it came time to provide program information, this rep droned on for fifteen minutes about all the features of the program offered. I could feel the prospect losing interest, and so could the salesperson. Instead of shutting up, the salesperson kept talking. The only thing he missed out was the color of the entrance door of the venue at the training venue!

After an exhausting Inform phase (which had been anything but simple!), the prospect said "I'd like some time to go over all of this, there's quite a lot to take in. Can you call me in a week or so?" Surprise surprise, he never heard from her again. He lost his prospect by overloading her with information in the final phase of the sale.

He failed to implement the Golden Rule of the Inform phase. It's critical to remember at this stage that if you want to close a deal, say less. Too much information can lead to paralysis.

When information is easy to understand, people are more likely to comprehend it, and even believe it. Persuasion researcher Robert Cialdini says, "When we grasp something *fluently* – that is, we can picture or process something quickly and effortlessly – we not only like that thing more, but also think it is more valid and worthwhile."[19]

The key here is to condense your offer's components as close to four succinct and digestible points as possible. You should present information in a way that avoids overwhelming the prospect with either too much information or complexity that might be stressful to process.

Our job is to make sure that the prospect views the offer and closing as a process that is both straightforward and painless. Introducing unnecessary details or choices.

Focus on emotional benefits

A key element of the Inform phase is using the facts we present to spell out how our prospects will benefit. Whenever we mention a fact about our offer, we must show our prospects what the tangible emotional benefit will be for them, and how this change will make them feel good.

This means that just presenting the bare details of our offer is not enough – we need to show off the positive emotional benefits behind the facts for that specific prospect. At this point, you know who they are and what motivates them. This means you know what would be entirely irrelevant to them and what the emotional benefits they would value are.

A useful way to make sure that what you are focusing on is relevant and valuable to the prospect is the "so what?" test. In short,

---

19 Cialdini, R. B. (2018). *Pre-suasion: A Revolutionary Way to Influence and Persuade*. Simon & Schuster Paperbacks.

whatever features or facts you're talking about, ask yourself "so what? Why would *this* prospect care? What's in it for them?" Think about how each feature helps the prospect gain something that leads to an emotional pay-off. Then make sure that you've followed up with that emotional benefit when you mention the feature.

For example: If you are selling a career-training program to a prospect who wants a sense of community and support from their training, you shouldn't just state, "You will attend two training sessions per month and we have a whole digital learning library". They have no reason to be interested in this by itself. Present it in terms they care about by showing them the answer to their "so what?".

Their focus is on community and support. This means that even if the digital learning library is amazing, they won't get any emotional benefit from it – though other prospects for the same offer might! The emotional benefit they are after is working in the same space with others.

Closer: "You'll have the opportunity to participate in two group training sessions per month, where you'll be able to connect with other participants, share ideas, and learn from each other, so you accelerate your learning and feel confident in the process."

By emphasizing the emotional benefits of the program for the prospect, we are more likely to capture the prospect's imagination and motivate them to take action. We are trying to help the prospect realize their own compelling logical and emotional reasons to make this positive life decision to commit to the offer. Highlighting the positive emotional benefits of the offer for that prospect makes the program feel more valuable and engaging, which ultimately increases the likelihood of a sale.

At this point, the prospect is probably going to be sold on your offer – the only thing left is to make sure they know how much it'll cost.

Discussing the price (oops... I mean "investment")

Every seasoned high-ticket closer knows that the last thing you want to do is drop the price bomb on your prospect too soon. Just like a magician saving their best trick for the finale, the price of your high-ticket offer should be revealed strategically and only when the time is right. After all, nobody wants to feel like they're being ambushed with a hefty price tag before they even have a chance to fully understand the value of your offer.

When we do our job right, the prospect will understand the full value of your offer to them specifically and will be motivated to sign up. Their motivation to find the money will be proportional to the work you've done. If paying is a big commitment, motivated prospects will be resourceful and find creative ways to finish a sale.

If a prospect says "no", it's either a result of a weak Interpretation or Inform phase – as a result, you've failed to help them find their compelling logical and emotional reasons – or they simply don't have the funds. That said, remember that in high-ticket sales, the prospects come to you. If they truly can't afford what we're selling, they won't let us get this far in the process – they won't even start the journey!

When discussing prices, one common mistake to avoid is overwhelming prospects with too many payment options at once. Stacking up choices for prospects to consider in the final phase of the sales process can lead to another case of analysis paralysis for the prospect and loss of control for you.

If we want to help the prospect, we can't ask them to make too many choices or offer too many options at once. It's important to stagger the options out and gauge the affordability of the prospect at each step. When I audit sales calls for my clients, I feel like pulling my hair out when I hear a supposed "high-ticket closer" put their foot in it by asking, "So Jane, would you like to go with the full-pay option or the six-pay option?"

High-ticket closers get paid on cash collected… why would you throw away a full-payment sale by presenting the payment plan option at the same time?!

In this example, instead of presenting all payment options at once, you could start by presenting the full pay option and asking the prospect how they plan to manage the investment. If they can afford it, you can move forward with closing the sale. If not, you can move on to the next payment plan and repeat the process until you find an option that works for them.

A useful way to guide prospects through this conversation is to discuss investments by asking *how* they can manage. The key word is "how," because prompting them to consider the "how" enables the prospect to think from a resourceful mindset.

Closer: "Jane, the investment for the program is $5,000. If I enroll you now, how would you manage your $5,000 investment?"

This reduces the focus for Jane down to one simple point: in what ways can she pay $5,000? If she can pay that directly, you can proceed directly to closing. If she cannot, she might have a workable solution already in mind or you could offer an alternative payment plan that suits her budget.

Once you get confirmation of their ability to afford it, you simply give your reasons why you think they will be a good fit for your offer and proceed with the assumptive close, "Jane, based on everything I've heard from you I feel confident you're a good fit, I'm just going to take your details to get you enrolled and then after that I'll explain your next steps…"

(Note the future pacing here).

The reason this works is due to the authority that you have established back in the Introduction and then maintained through using "Always Be Assessing" to present yourself as the person checking that the *prospect* is good for the offer (rather than the reverse). By assuming that they will close, you maintain that authority. At this point, the prospect will trust you and the product, and they will want to close.

There is no need to complicate things by presenting the prospect with a question you both already know the answer to!

The foundation of the Inform phase is clear and relevant communication with prospects. By keeping our message simple, we allow our prospects to experience maximum emotional engagement. When we provide this kind of experience for them, they are more likely to be motivated to sign up for the program.

You´ve made it to the summit – the end of the process. Now, from the top of the mountain, we can look back and admire all the hard work it took to arrive here.

My Inverse Closing™ process is rigorous, but keep in mind, you won't master it overnight. Like any other worthwhile skill, learning sales takes a lifetime of commitment. If you've gotten to this point in the book, maybe you're one of the special few who are willing to put in the work to become a high-ticket closing master.

Chapter 10

The Inverse Closing Method™ in action

Knowing the theory and steps behind the Inverse Closing Method™ alone is not enough. One of the catches is that for a high-ticket sales conversation it is almost impossible to write an exact script that will look the same every time. What it is about is listening to the clients carefully and moving through the phases step by step.

This is not a drawback – sounding like you are robotically following a script will damage your ability to establish yourself as an authority with the prospect. Instead, you need to be fully focused on listening actively and reacting to what the prospect is saying.

The best way to learn this is through experience. Recording and analyzing your calls afterwards is a brilliant way to look for what worked well and what you still need to improve.

What follows is a call that I analyzed with my mentees at the Cerra Closer Academy™. Read on for an authentic example of what the Inverse Closing Method™ looks like in action!

In this call, we are selling a high-ticket e-commerce offer which promises a complete done-for-you automated business. However, remember – this call isn't actually *about* e-commerce. What it's about is understanding our prospect – who they are, their issues and desires, while identifying and inoculating against any alternatives or barriers to closing the deal.

Introduction

We start by introducing ourselves and summarizing the product. However, at this moment, a large amount of background noise starts up on the prospect's end of the call. At this point, we can start to gently and politely start to initiate control of the conversation.

Closer: "There seems to be a lot of commotion in the background. It's really important to me that you're understanding all of this."

During a call, anything can happen. Do not be afraid at any point throughout the call to take a second to pause and check that they're still with you.

This politely and indirectly reminds them that this is a serious call that the prospect needs to pay attention to. It also helps to start establishing the status switch by which *you* are assessing *them* for their eligibility for the product, rather than the other way around. You then build on this like so.

Closer: "Right now, we are only bringing on just ten partners a month, just because it is a completely done-for-you service. This is as much as we can handle right now and that means we really want to make sure that we get things right. We do this by following a filtering process for our partnership applications.

One of the challenges is that sometimes partners that don't understand the industry and have unrealistic expectations sometimes try to interfere with our proven process – which you can understand causes problems for them. This means we're looking for certain qualities: someone who has an open mind, can be coached, and who has the discipline to stick to the core processes.

So, today is just for me to understand a little bit more about you and where you are and what you're looking for. Once I hear from you on those points that will give me an opportunity to talk about the partnership and how it works. At the end, I'll go away; take what I hear from you and present it to our team. Then I'll get back to you tomorrow so you'll know if it's something that we'd like to move forward with."

This point is vital – which is why we made sure that they were paying attention first. We are now shaping how the conversation will move from this point until the very end. If the prospect isn't listening, things are going to get lost and your job will only get more complicated.

By now, the prospect's ears will have perked up. They have realized that *they* are being assessed right now. If they want the help they came here to find, they need to be paying attention to you.

Investigation

From this moment, we can start moving into the Investigation phase – we have the prospect's attention and we're established as the authority in charge of the conversation, it's time to start gathering raw data.

Closer: "To begin with, it would be really useful to find out a little bit more about your background – where you are and what you're looking for here. So, what do you currently do for work?

In this case, it turns out that the prospect has two main sources of income: a hookah bar and his investments. At this point, there are several more data points you can fish for:

- How long have they owned the hookah bar?

- What are they investing in? Which industries?

- How much are they investing into their business and stock portfolio? How much are they making from it?

It also turned out that before moving to America, our prospect used to own a transportation business for five years. When he moved, however, he sold it on.

Another useful line of questioning is their experiences with the product or any similar product previously:

Closer: "Do you have any experience in the e-commerce space?"

In this case, the client doesn't have much – only basic information about Shopify and his own research. They do mention however that they do have a friend who has an e-commerce store – something to follow up on later in the interpretation.

Notice that at no point here am I asking any emotional questions or making any judgements. It can be very easy to jump on a detail and disappear down a rabbit hole – for example, examining in depth the issues about his business that he wants to automate away.

However, if you do this, you will lose track of the process and the conversation.

Gather all the raw data first, then use this to set the stage for the Interpretation phase that comes next.

An important data point we need to understand is our prospect's financial situation and their experiences with other competing products. In the interpretation phase, we will need to inoculate against any barriers and alternatives to accepting the offer. The earlier we learn about the issues which might get in the way of closing, the sooner we can start defending against them.

A particularly significant result from our questioning is that our prospect is currently looking at the real estate market – which means he is looking at making significant financial investments in the near future.

Interpretation

To sum up what we've learnt so far about our prospect:

- They own a business – a hookah bar

- They invest in the stock market as a second stream of income

- They have sold a previous business

- They know a little about e-commerce, however they are aware of the fact that you can use the tools without being competent

- They have a family that they are supporting with their income

In the interpretation, we can now start to dig a little deeper by asking follow-up questions and discovering more detailed information. For example, our discovery that the prospect had sold a previous business when they moved to America has two very important follow-up questions:

- What made you sell it?

- How much did you sell it for?

Over the Interpretation, we need to uncover more emotional and profound information than just the raw facts we found through the investigation. This emotional information falls into four categories:

- What is causing them pain right now?

- What do they want, but don't have right now?

- What reasons might they have to say "no" right now?

- What are their other options?

To cover this, we need to carefully ask Pain-evoking questions that draw their attention to why changing is their best option. We also need to subtly inoculate against any potential reasons we have identified they might not close.

Closer: "Now, we often find that the people we talk to have something in their situation that causes some sort of dissatisfaction or concern. Sometimes they're tired of trading their time for money or that they don't have any freedom from their career or business. Perhaps they want to spend more time with their family or doing something that they're more passionate about.

So, could you tell me: why is it important for you to change your situation and invest in something like this?"

The purpose of this question is to link the investigation to the interpretation and to prompt the prospect to start being more introspective about their own emotions. Remember, our focus isn't actually on the e-commerce solution we're selling here. It's on the prospect and their motivations.

Immediately, the prospect opens up and shares an issue. They want to support and provide for their family. However, their business is demanding that they work long hours – working weekends and late into the night.

This means that our next question has to evoke the emotions they are feeling about this. To reach the question, we reverse-engineer the desire: we want them to admit for themselves that they are frustrated about their lack of family time.

Closer: "Oh? So what does a typical day look like for you?"

With this question, we're inviting the prospect to talk us through their current situation – demonstrating the problems they face so we can drill deeper into them later. In this case, the prospect talks through their long hours – from eight in the morning to nine in the evening – and the huge pile of responsibilities they have to manage themselves.

Closer: "What is it that you don't like about that the most?"

At this point, the prospect might either highlight specific concerns about their work and business that frustrate them – perhaps they want more support with the hookah bar, but can't afford to bring on or train more staff. Drill into that as deeply as necessary – it is important data about their unresolved issues with their business. Use any data points from the investigation to support you in this.

Closer: "And your wife? Does she have any concerns about the situation?"

With this question, we are targeting their desire to spend more time with their family. In this case, the prospect opens up about how their wife is concerned about how they are always stressed. They also mention their frustrations, that often they don't ever get to spend time with their children – leaving before they are up and only getting back exhausted after they're in bed.

On top of this, asking this line of question inoculates against the possible objection that their wife might want to block the sale. If the prospect's wife is experiencing pain as a result of this issue as much as the prospect is, then she will be just as motivated to reach a solution. Helping the prospect realize this means they can move forward with confidence here.

Closer: "What is holding you back from spending more time with your family?"

This follows up on the previous line of questioning and the response reveals one of the prospect's key concerns: buying back his time.

The next thing to cover is alternatives to closing. In this case, there are several main points to inoculate against: their friend with e-commerce experience, their crypto investments, and their intended property purchase. If their preference is a more financially stable position, we need them to recognise that having an e-commerce store is the best way to achieve this. However, we also need to work out why they haven't just partnered up with their friend already.

Closer: "How long has our friend been running his e-commerce store?"

This gives us the opportunity to start bringing the conversation around to their friend. This pays off when it turns out that the prospect's interest is due to their friend's success in e-commerce.

Closer: "Have you approached them to show how to set an e-commerce store up? Why haven't you asked them to help you?"

The objection we are aiming to inoculate against is the prospect deciding that, while an e-commerce store is exactly the solution they need, their friend can help them much better than we could. If this were the case, they'd have partnered up already! In this case, it turns out that the prospect's friend is apparently always too busy to discuss it.

The prospect strongly believes that his friend is just afraid that if they share their secrets, they'll have to share the profits with the prospect – rather than keeping it all to themselves! With that in mind, the friend doesn't look like they'll want to help the prospect much at all.

Closer: "Have you thought about investing more in crypto?"

This question targets the possibility of the prospect focusing their investments on crypto over paying for our e-commerce solution. In this case, the prospect is not interested in building their investments here since they have already decided it is not secure enough.

Closer: "And what about real estate investments? You mentioned you were looking at properties – what's holding you back there?"

This shifts the conversation onto property as a natural progression from other investments. The prospect corrects us a little – they're just looking for one property, rather than investing in several. Their issue there is that it requires a lot of capital and your money is tied up for many years before you see a return on your investment.

Remember – the prospect has come to us. There will be a reason why they were interested in your offer. What we are doing here is inoculating them against the alternatives by getting them to remind themselves of the reasons your offer was valuable enough they would approach you.

Other avenues to pursue here include the frustration of struggling to find a house and the costs of making a down payment.

Implication

At this point, we are onto the Implication. We need to remind the prospect of how their pain points are causing suffering and that they need to act urgently to fix things soon. If they do so, then their life will improve.

By this point, we know their issues and pain points:

- They are trying to provide for their family

- Their business is not offering the income and security they need

- They are frustrated by how closely tied they are to their business – it demands most of their time and energy

- They do not get to spend as much time as they would like with their family because they have to focus so much on their work

For the negative implication, we need to remind them of how things need to change.

Closer: "So you mentioned that you're spending all of your time bound to your business just to make ends meet. You're so busy providing for your family that you don't actually get to enjoy spending time with them, going on holidays and so on.

Fast forward a few years. Imagine this. You're still overworked, overstressed, and your family hasn't seen you properly in weeks. Where does that leave you?"

This paints a stark picture of what is waiting for the prospect if nothing changes. By this point, they admit that the current status quo isn't serving them at all.

On the other hand, our e-commerce automation has a lot to offer them. In the positive implication, we need to help them imagine this.

Closer: "Imagine now that you had an e-commerce business that was running and it was generating the money that you wanted. You could now go away, and not worry about the business and actually enjoy that precious time with your kids and family. In fact, you can do that as many times in the year as you wanted and it doesn't impact you.

Now, tell me, if you're in that situation, how would that look differently for you?"

Asking them to imagine this brighter future, the prospect relaxes as they admit why this is truly valuable to them.

Prospect: "I'll be free"

Inform

From here, everything is straightforward. We now know a lot about our prospect and what would motivate them to accept our offer of a fully automated done-for-you e-commerce business.

- They want a stable and reliable source of income to support their family

- They feel trapped by their current business which is not providing what they need

- They want the freedom to spend time with their family

- They are very conscious that their wife and family are worried about how much time they spend working and the amount of stress they are under

- They have looked elsewhere – their friend who already has e-commerce experience – but have not received the support they needed

This means that the features of our offer that they will find most relevant need to address these pain points:

- This done-for-you e-commerce business will easily produce a passive income that will support the business and the prospect's family

- As this offer is an automated done-for-you business, it will require zero time and attention from the prospect – allowing them to enjoy their new-found freedom with their wife and children

- This offer is provided by experts dedicated to helping their clients succeed, ensuring that our prospect has all the support they need to get started

Once these points have been presented, the final step is to help the prospect work out how they will make the investment. In this case, we already know – the profits from having sold their previous business will cover this.

We arrange the deposit payment and get them to sign the agreement, then start organizing the next steps. This includes wiring details for the full balance and booking their onboarding call with the fulfillment team.

At this point, we've managed to carry the ball over the line – the prospect has agreed to close! Now there's nothing to do but look forward to the tidy commission check we just earned and polish our skills in order to perform even better on the next call!

Chapter 11

Commit
to Mastery

If the basic phases of the Inverse Closing Method™ were all you needed to become a master high-ticket closer, you could put this book down right now. Unfortunately, it doesn't quite work that way. As we discussed in Chapter 4, high-ticket selling is a skillful process. You can't learn and master a skill just by learning about the theory from a book.

Becoming a master in any profession requires more than a single book, lecture, or program. Like all worthwhile skills, mastering high-ticket closing takes a lifetime of practice. Your progress will never finish, but every moment of practice will be better than the last. After having invested a lifetime, the rewards of your mastery will leave others in awe.

Take it from one of the world's most recognizable masters, Pablo Picasso.

The price of mastery

In 1960s Paris, a young woman from the countryside ambled down Rue Cler, taking in the joyful bustle, when a particular old man caught her attention.

Oh my God, thought the woman. *That's Pablo Picasso!*

Stunned, she gravitated toward the famous artist as if he were the center of the universe. Hovering over Picasso's shoulder, she couldn't muster the words to greet him. Picasso's cafe companions noticed the young woman and frowned.

Picasso's shining head rotated like an owl's. His impassive eyes met the young woman's eager expression.

"Mr. Picasso," the young woman blurted too loud, alarming the surrounding cafe-goers. "Please…"

She snatched a napkin from a nearby table and shoved it toward the artist.

"Would you make me a sketch?" she practically screamed. Picasso's friends rolled their eyes.

A stern woman next to the pair said, "Please, we're trying to enjoy our coffee."

The young woman hung her head, embarrassed at her inability to control her volume around a celebrity. When she looked up at the famous painter to apologize, though, she was surprised at what she saw. Picasso was smiling.

"It's alright," Picasso said. He took a pen out of his shirt pocket and made a few quick lines on the napkin. He handed the napkin back to the young woman. She looked at what the old master drew. In her hands she held a sketch of a joyful songbird, presented in Picasso's inimitable style. The blue ink of his pen nearly leapt off the humble napkin.

The young woman was amazed. The artist managed to achieve such clarity and meaning in a work he'd only spent a few moments putting together.

"Now," Picasso said, "that will be a million francs."

The young woman couldn't help but laugh. When she looked at the artist, though, he wasn't laughing along with her. In fact, he now seemed quite serious. The young woman didn't know what to say.

"But, sir... are you serious?" she asked. Picasso nodded his head. She was flabbergasted. She thought the artist had made this drawing out of the goodness of his heart.

"But... but..." she stammered, "but you drew this in only thirty seconds!" Picasso looked her dead in the eye.

"No, my dear," said Picasso, "it took me seventy years to draw that bird."

For Picasso, his artistic skill was not a parlor trick for cafe crowds. It was not a hobby or a side hustle. Art was his life. To become one of the world's most famous and successful artists, Picasso made a lifelong commitment to improving his technique. Each work of art Picasso produced was imbued with years of sweat, study, and strategy.

As a great artist dedicates himself to refinement throughout his career, so too should doctors, pilots, and salespeople. Being truly great at any skill requires tenacity. There is a mantra often repeated by the most talented people in all walks of life. To be the best, you have to...

Put in the work

It's no secret that hard work separates the greats from the pretenders. Unfortunately, most salespeople never accomplish sales mastery because they don't put in the work. It's human nature to grow bored, lose interest, and settle for mediocrity. The road to greatness is arduous, and most people don't care to put in the effort to travel it. If you don't have the drive to be the greatest seller in the world, that's okay.

My Inverse Closing Method™ you've learned in this book will still help you succeed at sales anyway. However, if you want to achieve the highest level, to reach the summit of sales, you must be willing to outwork everyone else.

One reason many salespeople fail to invest the required effort is because their conception of sales is all wrong. When we treat sales as a selfish, transactional endeavor, there isn't much incentive to be great at it – who wants to master a skill nobody else appreciates? In reading this book, you've already given yourself a leg up because you've seen there can be a different approach.

Knowing the theory is a very different thing to having put in the time and effort to get practical experience. It can be overwhelming to consider the amount of time it takes to become a master. However, gaining practical experience is the fun part. When we notice ourselves improving, we become more self-confident, determined, and optimistic we will reach our ultimate goal.

To master Inverse Closing™, salespeople must undergo three distinct phases of learning. As we progress through these phases, we hone our techniques and develop comprehension for the craft that will take us to the upper echelon.

Hindsight, insight, foresight

Selling, like art, is a skill that requires continuous development to master. When we succeed at high-ticket closing, it seems like we're simply having a conversation. It doesn't appear difficult to an outside observer. However, beneath the surface, there are subtle nuances of conversation, silent persuasion techniques, and an invisible framework the salesperson follows to guide his prospect toward a sale.

As the young woman was baffled by Picasso's insistence on a million francs for a doodle scribbled on a napkin, high-ticket closing can appear to be easy on the surface. Of course, anyone who has tried a career in sales knows there's nothing easy about it, and the world of high-ticket takes things to a new level. To be a high-ticket closer who is sought after time and time again we must track market changes and adapt to an ever-evolving community of buyers.

A good high-ticket closer is like a swan gliding across the top of the water – their legs churn wildly under the surface, but on top, the process looks calm and effortless.

To move through our process as gracefully as the swan, we must put in the time to learn how to make the difficult task of sales look easy. There are three stages to mastering the art and science of high-ticket selling. They are hindsight, insight, and foresight.

In sport, there's a phenomenon that occurs when a talented player moves from the amateur level to the professional ranks. Even if a soccer player has all the athletic ability and knowledge of the game necessary to succeed, when she's a rookie, she will make mistakes. Consequently, more experienced players will run circles around her. After spending time on the pitch, the game will eventually "slow down" for her, and her natural talents will shine through.

Here's how we slow down the game of high-ticket selling in three stages:

1. Hindsight

Hindsight is the understanding we gain about a situation after it occurs. Its meaning is encapsulated by the phrase, "If I knew then what I know now…" Hindsight usually consists of information that would have been crucial *during* the event, but for whatever reason, it wasn't available. Hindsight helps us see why certain situations happened, how they happened and what could have happened differently.

People gather hindsight while learning a new skill to gain familiarity about situations they commonly find themselves in. Our rookie soccer player reviews game footage to observe the mistakes she made during practice. Her coach can point out potential passes she missed and when she let a goal-scoring opportunity slip away. Likewise, we record our calls and listen to them with a coach, or a more experienced high-ticket closing expert, to gather hindsight.

When we are first learning a new skill, we must accept we'll make mistakes and learn from them when an expert points them out.

High-ticket closing masters-in-training won't be able to close every sale. Still, we must accept responsibility for losing sales and gather hindsight about why we lost them; this will motivate us to improve.

Having frameworks and structures to follow is a good way to start learning without making constant mistakes. These frameworks are usually directly based on an expert's mastery of the processes. Using their hindsight and hard-earned experience, they've worked out the methods and tricks that you need to perform well.

Inverse Closing™ itself is an example of this for example. I've taken everything I've learnt as a high-ticket closer and coaching others myself and broken the process down into repeatable steps. A common mistake to be careful with when relying on frameworks however is skipping steps.

A beginner doesn't have the experience and understanding to benefit from hindsight when using a framework. They sometimes might not even notice when an element of the process gets cut short or jumped over entirely!

For example, we might instinctively jump to the Interpretation phase when our prospect tells us about their dissatisfaction with their situation in the Introduction phase, rather than sticking to the process and gathering all the foundational intelligence we need. Or we may find ourselves jumping the gun and skipping to the Information phase before we've completed a thorough Interpretation and Implication, preventing us from effectively motivating prospects toward a sale.

Following a framework can help a closer build the experience to start benefiting from their own hindsight more. When we put words to the different parts of the process, as we've done in the preceding chapters, it helps us see exactly where we're going wrong. The more we follow the framework, the closer to second nature it becomes.

Eventually, you reach a point where a framework alone is no longer enough. After all, learning through hindsight can come from our own experience or from the experience of others. Like an artist studies the old masters to enrich their palette, we too can study from the masters of the high-ticket craft.

One of the most effective ways to do this is to have an expert listen to our recorded sales calls. This expert closer can give tailored feedback to the learner, and provides a clear indication of how to deal with prospects next time.

After completing their theoretical training, new high-ticket closers in my Academy are matched with a coach who helps them apply their skills in practice. During coaching sessions, the coach carefully reviews recordings of their sales calls, analyzing everything from call structure to questioning techniques. This process enables the high-ticket closers to learn from their mistakes and gain valuable insights. By recognizing and analyzing errors, they gain valuable hindsight and improve their sales skills.

2. Insight

The next stage of learning is insight. Hindsight allows us to learn from situations in the past and provides us with the knowledge we need for situations in the present. When we gather hindsight from previous practice and use it to build an action plan for the present, the information becomes insight.

Insight gives us a deep understanding of a situation, which helps us determine decisions in the moment. Instead of only noticing or understanding something *after* it's happened, insight means we are aware of and understand what is going on *when* it is actually happening.

Eventually, the soccer rookie takes the learnings of her training and game-tape review and implements them out on the pitch. She remembers her coach's words about taking a chance on a through ball and commits to making the play. Likewise, she sees when to follow her team captain's advice and go for a slide tackle. She learns to make out windows of opportunity previously invisible to her.

Hindsight becomes insight through repetition. As a musician learns the scales to play the piano, high-ticket closers repeat the sales process to learn the intricacies of how it works. Once we've applied enough repetition, we can adjust in the moment, not wait for a success or failure.

In high-ticket sales, we need to stay flexible and able to adapt – to be a sales master, we have to be able to sell to anyone. Unfortunately, everyone is different and each requires attention that is specifically tailored to their challenges and emotions. This is where insight becomes invaluable.

When we practice our technique with my Inverse Closing Method™, we learn to adjust our own strategy instinctually. High-ticket closers can develop a sense for when to turn up the heat and when to shut up and listen.

We learn when to motivate a hesitant prospect who's expressed worries, and when to extricate more intelligence from a prospect who seems to be a surefire sale on the surface. We can interpret deeper context from simple sentences our prospects say in passing and use it to close the toughest of sales.

The insight phase is all about developing the ability to react in the moment to the information we have to guide our prospects through the process. When we arrive at the insight phase, we learn we must have a rationale behind everything we say and do. Our insight helps us know what to ask and what to listen for. We refine our approach and become more efficient high-ticket closers, rather than spending all our energy trying to dazzle prospects with manipulative tactics.

We can speed up the development of insight by working with a broad range of prospects. Every prospect is unique, and learning how to navigate different backstories helps us gain insight for any situation.

When we've gained the insight to change course in real time, the sales game slows down to a point where we can dictate the pace of the game ourselves, rather than following and reacting to someone else's pacing. Achieving this means we've reached near-mastery.

3. Foresight

The final stage of sales mastery is foresight. Once we have the ability to learn from mistakes in the hindsight stage and react in the moment in the insight stage, we're ready to build up our anticipatory abilities and intuition – allowing us to guide the process and take charge more easily.

We'll be able to predict how we want the conversation to go with just a little information about the prospect. Then, we can use our foresight to take precautions (think of them as mental knee pads), which limit our chances of getting hurt when it's time to make the pitch.

Gaining foresight means we can see what is going to happen next. As we gradually build up our intuition, we can see what will happen at each moment of the process before it begins. Foresight doesn't help us determine whether a coin will come up heads, which horse will win the race, or who's going to break first in a staring contest between strangers. Foresight isn't guessing – it's the ability to understand where your prospects are and where they need to be to have them ready for a close from just moments into the sales process.

When our soccer rookie – now a master herself – has developed foresight, she gains the ability to read the field and approximate what is going to happen next long before it actually does. She has seen it all before so many times, it's impossible to surprise her. This lets her spot a goal-scoring opportunity and grab it before anyone else on the pitch.

The only way to gain foresight is through experience. It takes thousands of sales calls and an ironclad commitment to learn from our mistakes. It takes years, but once we reach this phase, our sales ability reaches unseen heights. Foresight allows us to see exactly how to guide prospects in the most effective way, every time. To get to this stage, you need to have had mentorship. You don't get to be Obi Wan without having Yoda to guide you first!

Learn from the best

Working alongside a masterful mentor is the key to gathering information to build the learning process from hindsight to insight to foresight. Mentors have seen all kinds of crazy situations, and they're willing to share the lessons they learned. This means that a mentor can help guide and support you on the journey towards mastering the skills behind high-ticket closing.

I learned the value of a mentor when I was in the midst of a devastating sales slump.

"What can I do?" I asked.

Seamus then gave me two monumental pieces of advice. They've rung in my ears for years now. The first piece of advice shocked me.

"First of all," he said, "you've gotta not give a shit whether they sign or not."

"What?" I said, "but that's the whole point!"

"Yes," he continued. "But you want it so much, you reek of desperation. Don't worry about whether they sign. Just do your job. They'll follow you where you want 'em to go."

I nodded my head. Then Seamus gave me the second piece of advice – one that has informed my entire approach to sales ever since.

"Sales isn't a tug-of-war," he said. "It's about puttin' your arm around someone's shoulder, goin' for a walk, seein' the sights."

I had never heard sales described this way. From that moment, my conception of what sales could be totally shifted. It was not about me convincing my prospects to buy. It was about allowing them to sell themselves. This revelation – that sales is not an adversary interaction – is a core part of how I approach sales and how I teach others to view closing to this day.

In addition to the wisdom he provided, my time with Seamus taught me a profound lesson about how to master sales: an essential part of the journey to sales mastery is mentorship.

This includes learning from a mentor and – after achieving mastery – becoming one.

Mentorship is perhaps as old as human thought. Ancient philosophers all had mentors to guide them on their paths toward enlightenment. Aristotle learned from Plato, who learned from Socrates. In the modern world, the best athletes all have masterful coaches.

The true test of mastery comes from the ability to teach others. Great coaches never end up coaching bad teams. If they join a team with low stats from the years before they signed on, it's only a matter of time before the team's record turns around.

No matter how a team performed before, they will inevitably improve as long as they take the master's lessons. It's no coincidence that on any list of the greatest coaches in any sport, you'll find they've all coached the best players.

Sales is no different from any professional skill, all of which require mentorship to master. If we take them seriously, mentorships can open our eyes to new possibilities – learning from the best can be its own reward. The key to successful high-ticket sales is skill – a willingness to learn, develop, and earn mastery is a key trait for any high-ticket closer.

Indeed, all the closers at my high-ticket sales agency – even those who have been working with me for nearly four years now – still turn up to my sales coaching sessions with pen and pad to take on new insights and lessons. You're never too experienced to learn something new – high-ticket closing in particular is a craft where there is always something you can fine tune!

Sadly, because so many salespeople have a fundamentally flawed view of the sales process, it's difficult to find a good mentor. When searching for the ideal mentor, a salesperson can seek someone with a good sales track record, but a history of selling doesn't equate to a good trainer.

What's more important is to find an expert salesperson who applies the right approach. This doesn't mean a potential mentor must have read this book (although it wouldn't hurt!). Rather, it means finding a mentor who treats their craft seriously, not as a transactional game, will yield great results.

The best mentors will challenge us to be our best selves. They provide an answer for everything, especially when we make mistakes. They ask insightful questions to help us understand what we're doing right, and most importantly, what we're doing wrong.

Remember that hindsight and learning from mistakes are invaluable learning tools. To be the best high-ticket closers, it's crucial we know what *doesn't* work. When we're looking for a mentor, we must keep in mind we want someone who can tell us what *not* to do. We can't develop our skills by only seeing what we do well – we need someone to help us notice what we're doing wrong and the mistakes we're making.

We also want to make sure our mentors share knowledge from a place of experience. Steve Jobs said the problem with consultants is they have never made the mistakes themselves. The best mentors have the scars to prove the mistakes they've made. They can help us avoid the same errors.

I trusted Seamus' advice because he had a track record full of success *and* failure to back up his advice. Everything he knew, he had learnt through experience the hard way.

Becoming a master requires a balance of knowledge and wisdom, both of which can be shared by a master. While we may have the requisite knowledge to be a successful closer, a mentor provides additional wisdom to fill in our knowledge gaps.

The difference between knowledge and wisdom is the same as the difference between theory and practice. While theory is born of the intellect, practice is born of experience. Likewise, knowledge is intellectual while wisdom is experiential. It comes from learning hard truths in the real world. So when we find a mentor to guide us, we must cherish them and their failures, so we might learn how to avoid the same missteps.

Empty your cup

The key to implementing the Inverse Closing Method™ is to strip away everything you were taught before reading this book and shift your mindset to accommodate what you've learned. Bruce Lee told his trainees, "In order to taste my water, you must first empty your cup."

We all have preconceived ideas that keep us from reaching our fullest potential, whether in business or in life. We might think we are incapable of running our own company because we don't have the right qualifications to be an entrepreneur. We might feel we don't deserve to have a loving and fulfilling marriage because we aren't good enough. Or, we might think we shouldn't look for a new job because we prefer our uncomfortable status quo over the unknown.

There are countless preconceived ideas in sales holding the industry back. Many see sales as tacky, selfish, and useless. Salespeople don't receive the respect they deserve because of the bad actors who approach sales all wrong.

However, this book offers a new perspective on the sales process and a new approach to doing it – high-ticket sales. We have redefined what it means to sell, and have opened up the door for people to enjoy sales as a rewarding career. High-ticket sales can be noble, helpful, and beneficial to society and this is why I love it.

Shifting our mindset to a new conception of sales to become a high-ticket closer can be painful because it means abandoning the life we know. People don't like to change. However, if we don't, we won't ever overcome the old, flawed, painful approaches to sales.

Traditional sales can be a frustrating and confrontational role in which you are forced to always be closing to prospects who just don't want to know. Add to that the fact that there is so little support for development – you get treated as though you either have the right personality or you don't. Just how sustainable would a long-term career in those conditions be?

Imagine now that you have a role that is collaborative and supportive. The people you are selling to not only want to talk to you, but they are genuinely excited about how you can help them. You make a positive impact on their life at the same time working anywhere in the world with just a laptop and earning what a doctor does. On top of this, it is possible to find the guidance and mentorship to learn and grow – becoming the best closer you can possibly be. What would a job like that give you what you don't have now?

(See what I just did here? When I say that the persuasive skills Inverse Closing™ teaches are good for more than just closing, I'm not kidding!)

By reading this book, you've already started to shift. While shifting your mindset is essential, so too is understanding the practicalities behind breaking into the world of High-ticket closing.

Getting hired as a high-ticket closer

When it comes to finding high-ticket jobs, there are several routes that you could take. The "standard" route might be going through recruitment websites such as Indeed, for example, and searching for high-ticket closer roles. Another might be taking the freelancing route – such as through job post boards – and building a relationship from there.

These methods are not always ideal, however, and have their drawbacks.

As the star of high-ticket rises, employers hiring for traditional sales roles might misapply the term "high-ticket closer" – using it incorrectly as a synonym for "brilliant salesperson". Using Google and generic websites to find high-ticket roles needs to be done with caution.

The other issue arises when those without a high-ticket skill set find themselves in a high-ticket role. A salesperson might successfully present themselves as an expert – claiming they have done a million-dollars-worth of sales successfully for example – without having committed to mastering high-ticket. Having promised the world, the entrepreneur puts them on the phones. The problem is that – as I have stressed throughout this book – a traditional sales approach is inadequate for high-ticket.

Too often I see the costs of this. The entrepreneur does not realize their mistake until their new closer has burnt through and wasted

20 or 30 leads – by which time it's too late. Once a prospect has had one bad experience, they are not likely to want to invest in the product. If they have been burnt once, they lose faith in the entrepreneur – even if it was not directly the entrepreneur's fault.

This is a problem. In high-ticket, each lead costs the entrepreneur to establish. In Chapter 2, I described the process by which a prospect is led towards the sales call and a purchase. This process costs $150 to $300 per lead.

This means that an entrepreneur with experience in high-ticket sales will want to be careful about who they take on as a high-ticket closer. They need someone who can have high-value conversations with their audience, maintain their integrity and not tarnish their brand by using inappropriate or manipulative approaches. As a high-ticket closer, your job is to show entrepreneurs that you fit the bill.

Fortunately, there are communities built around high-ticket that you can turn to for work opportunities. The option that I find most effective are Facebook forums that you can join for free.

Entrepreneurs who understand what the role of high-ticket closer is and the skills required will use these forums as a venue to share their details and that they are looking for a high-ticket closer. As they understand what this role requires, their requirements will be close enough to the reality that most traditional salespersons will not automatically qualify.

The task in front of you here is successfully standing out from the crowd and presenting yourself as an authentic high-ticket closer committed to mastering the skill set and achieving excellence in the role.

How to stand out from the crowd

So, how can you set yourself apart as someone who knows what they are doing from day one, rather than some run-of-the-mill salesperson?

First, you need to understand what the entrepreneur is looking for. They will be an individual who has put a phenomenal amount of blood, sweat, and tears into a product that they need to sell. Each possible lead is valuable to them – because each prospect is prequalified, simply generating leads is expensive. The entrepreneur is not able to have these sales conversations themselves – either they do not have the time and energy for sales in addition to their other roles in their business, or they have no sales ability.

Therefore, they are looking for someone who can have a conversation with their audience while preserving their brand and integrity. They will *want* you, as a skilled high-ticket closer, to solve their problem. Your challenge is to persuade them that you actually are someone who can and will help them – not some dodgy salesperson who will *hurt* their reputation or waste their carefully cultivated leads.

Does this sound familiar?

Getting a role as a high-ticket closer is a high-ticket conversation in its own right with the entrepreneur as the prospect.

You can demonstrate your mastery of high-ticket *through* your interactions with the entrepreneur. Your goal is not to demonstrate that you could sell anything to anyone, but that you understand the avatar of their ideal prospect well enough that you can have the conversation which will help convince their prospect to buy.

This will require you to do research on the entrepreneur and their brand beforehand – while being able to ask amazing questions in the interview is valuable, having anticipated the answers to some of those questions beforehand will genuinely impress the entrepreneur.

- **Who is the audience?**

  Who are the prospects the entrepreneur expects you to talk with? This is a good opportunity to demonstrate your understanding of the kind of person you expect to be talking to – what matters to them, what their life and experiences might be like. It also gives you a chance to demonstrate your mastery of the skills that form the Investigation phase.

- **What problem does your offer solve?**

  What value will the prospect get from buying? A conversation about a subscription to an investment mastermind will be very different compared to one offering business support for single mothers building a business from home. Showing an awareness of who the prospects are in addition to why they want the entrepreneur's product and the benefit they will receive proves you understand the value of the high-ticket item to the prospect – demonstrating the skills behind the Interpretation phase.

- **What are the main objections?**

  The point of the Investigation and Interpretation phases are to help identify what could hold the prospect back from buying. Being able to intelligently discuss the main objections that a prospect might have and present how you might overcome them before they come up – is a skill the entrepreneur will find immensely valuable.

Understanding the prospect's problem, avatar, and possible objections inside and out is the hardest part of the high-ticket sales call. If you are able to outline these in bullet points and provide an interview that demonstrates you understand how to have a conversation around them, the entrepreneur *will* offer you the job.

What you are doing here is demonstrating lateral thinking – a good high-ticket salesperson is able to listen carefully while connecting the dots and reading between the lines. If you can demonstrate other instances of having displayed insight that lets you probe for information (without misstepping or causing offense), unravel the issue, then springboard to the solution in a way that encourages the prospect to discover your solution without feeling manipulated, you are demonstrating high-ticket sales mastery.

Being able to demonstrate reputable training as to how to do high-ticket sales will also count in your favor. I find that those who have completed my high-ticket sales training program tend to find themselves at the front of the queue when looking for work.

You can find out more about how to get involved with my programs by scanning the QR code below:

Scan me!

When looking for training, it is important to have a program that offers structured guidance and mentorship. My Cerra Closer Academy™ is broken down into four components:

1. Online learning, with modules teaching the core skills and concepts of Inverse Closing™.

2. Buddy-up system, in which you shadow a veteran high-ticket closer, which lets you mirror their successes and learn from their example.

3. One-to-one coaching, in which a Inverse Closing™ coach gives you direct and personalized feedback on your recorded sales calls.

4. Group coaching, typically run by myself, in which we focus on the bigger picture high-level concepts.

Having completed these four components, we offer a certification. Being provided with a reputable certification is invaluable, as it allows you a means to prove that you have been putting time and effort into your personal development as a high-ticket closer.

Also, by demonstrating an appetite for self-improvement and personal development you are going to be upholding the values that so many of these entrepreneurs live by which is a massive bonus.

Identifying an opportunity worth chasing

When you find yourself in an interview for a high-ticket role, it is not just a one-way process. You should make sure to ask questions that allow you to assess the quality of the opportunity from your perspective.

Examples of what to ask about include:

- **The product itself**
  This is worth researching outside of the interview as well. An established product with positive reviews is far easier to sell. If it is a product that you would be happy to buy, then it is far easier to present it as a solution to the prospect. It can be common for a company to try and present a low-value product as high-ticket.

  Trying to persuade someone that something has value when you wouldn't touch it with a ten-foot pole makes your life unnecessarily difficult and embarrassing. Make sure it is something worth selling by ensuring that the offer has been sold before to demonstrate proof of concept. You want to start furthest away from the bottom of the hill.

- **Their sales process and funnel**
  High-ticket sales has a specific approach to how prospects are nurtured and brought in. It is far better to work with a company that has a sophisticated funnel tailored to attract and nurture their ideal client – this guarantees that you will get a constant flow of engaged prospects who are interested in the product, rather than a supply which quickly goes quiet as initial interest dries up.

  You could be the Picasso of high-ticket sales – a genius of sales – and it won't matter if the leads are terrible or nonexistent! Imagine how ridiculous it would be to be asked to sell a dating coaching program to a nun who'd sworn a vow of celibacy! If the leads are low quality and the funnel isn't aligned to the ideal client, you could end up looking like you're performing poorly when it isn't at all your fault!

- **How are sales calls presented to the prospect**
  There is nothing more awkward than a call in which the prospect is expecting something wildly different. It's important to be on the lookout for bait-and-switch tactics or false promises. When evaluating a companies' sales funnel, look for transparency and authenticity in their messaging and approach. After investing 45 minutes in a sales call, the last thing you want to hear is a surprised and disappointed prospect say, "I thought this was free".

- **The entrepreneur's recruitment history**
  Nobody wants to operate in a bad work environment. It is always a good idea to establish why the entrepreneur is hiring and what staff retention is like.

- **Commissions**
  Since commission is how a high-ticket closer gets paid, make sure there is an official structure around how commissions work. Typically speaking, commission payouts should be made out once the cooling off period is over. This typically is somewhere between 14 to 30 days and typically commissions are ten percent of the cash collected for a sale.

- **Paperwork and contracts**
  This ties into the previous point, but a good contract protects both you and your employer. A well-written contract defines and protects the structure in which you are working.

Improving the World Through High-Ticket Closing

As technology advances, sales will change with it. Recent advances in AI have certainly shaken things up – there is concern that the role of salesperson will be replaced.[20] New technologies and generative AIs make it easier than ever to automate human interaction.

Traditional sales is a simple and predictable interaction. It is simply advertising a service and pushing the prospect to buy. This simplicity makes it easy to program a chatbot to automate the process – something incredibly valuable for a company looking to

---

20 Cook, M. (2018, January 2). *Why Artificial Intelligence Will Eliminate Millions Of Sales Jobs.* Forbes. https://www.forbes.com/sites/forbesagencycouncil/2018/01/02/why-artificial-intelligence-will-eliminate-millions-of-sales-jobs/

Kijko, P. (2021, September 27). *Will AI Replace Salespeople? Opinions Differ Between Experts in the Industry.* HackerNoon. https://hackernoon.com/will-ai-replace-salespeople-opinions-differ-between-experts-in-the-industry

cut costs while putting as many offers in front of as many potential customers as possible.

Automating sales roles means that a company might only need a handful of staff where they used to need an entire sales department. Rather than having a full team who are limited to only work hours, a computer could be active 24/7, performing a whole range of tasks and chores which only really require an ability to communicate.

Honestly, some things are so straight-forward, they don't need an AI at all! A sufficiently well-designed webpage or FAQ could do them. Imagine how much better they could operate if powered by AI as well!

On top of this, the general public might *welcome* the ability to cut out the salesperson entirely – freeing themselves from the painfully awkward cliché of the hard sell and salesperson who won't take "no" for an answer.

Cutting out the salesperson

Ten years ago, my friend Jane had a terrible experience buying a car. A pushy salesman threw the entire book of manipulative tactics at her, upsold her at every turn, and left her feeling slimy as she drove off the lot.

"Nice car!" I remarked when she pulled up to meet me for lunch.

"Thanks," she said. "It's the last one I'll ever buy from a dealership."

Last year, Jane was ready to upgrade her ride again, so she did what everyone does when faced with a challenge today: she went online. She spent two weeks knee-deep in car reviews on YouTube and scrolled through car-selling websites for hours after work. She knew the blue book value of every midsize sedan on the market. She decided to purchase through a car-buying mobile app and made her choice on a Friday afternoon. After a few taps, the car was on its way. By Monday morning, Jane had her new ride parked in her driveway.

Not once did she come close to talking with a salesperson.

Salespeople's outdated tactics have caused our culture to cut them out. Buyers have caught on to every gimmick and trick a salesperson can employ. Consumers are more wary than ever, and are experts at sniffing out an unwanted salesperson.

Rather than changing their approach, traditional salespeople have doubled down on the same tired tactics. They keep using the expected approach, but they try to be sneakier about it. This only deepens feelings of mistrust from consumers.

While this might be a concern for the traditional sales approach, I don't see this happening for high-ticket sales any time soon. This is mostly down to the fact that high-ticket sales is defined by a more complex emotional and human connection, as well as a comprehensive understanding of human behavior and how we make decisions. There is no way that AI will be replicating that any time soon!

Traditional sales has an unfortunate tendency to focus on charisma and the ability to communicate over skill – training and personal development aren't focuses. This means that, without any unique human skills behind it, traditional sales is uniquely vulnerable to AI and automation. Once we produce an AI which automates a traditional sales approach, the jobs themselves are going to just disappear.

High-ticket, on the other hand, is all about skill, higher-level conversation, and human intuition rather than regurgitating information about a product. Remember our definition from Chapter 4: Selling is the skillful process of directing a prospect's attention to their own compelling reasons (logic), evoking powerful emotions, with the aim of facilitating a positive buying decision.

No matter how good the AI is right now, this is not a skillset that can be easily automated. A computer might be able to gather the facts, but a computer can't pick up on the subtle cues to work out the emotional motivators that might push someone to buy. A computer can't share vulnerability to build a connection or read the room to work out what it should or shouldn't mention.

This means that, thanks to its complexity, high-ticket sales stands to be a safe haven for professional salespeople who are concerned about being put out of work by AI. While it might happen in the distant future, modern AI is utterly incapable of reproducing the intuition and subtlety that high-ticket demands – especially while talking in real time.

Industry is only going to grow

The high-ticket industry certainly isn't going to go anywhere. As technology progresses, people are learning that their experience and knowledge have a value that can't be replaced – this means that information is becoming one of the most significant commodities on the market.

ELearning is certainly going to become one of the quickest ways to make money. High-ticket closers are going to be in demand in order to sell these eLearning products to the world.

As eLearning grows, high-ticket sales are going to grow with it. Since Covid, the world has woken up to the power of eLearning. More and more people recognise the power of learning with online courses these days – for example, the European eLearning market is expected to grow by $28 billion between 2020 and 2024,[21] a staggering amount for just four years!

High-ticket skills outside of sales

Mastering a high-ticket skill set is about more than unlocking professional opportunities – it benefits your life in many surprising ways. After all, you are always selling *something*, whether you realize it or not.

Many things in life are about communication, persuading others, and presenting opportunities and solutions. Whether it is in your relationships, in the workplace, or the countless interactions that come up over the course of your day, having strong communicative skills are going to help you succeed and help everyone around you to succeed as well.

---

21 E-Learning Industry Overview - Market Growth, Trends and Forecast Market Analysis. (n.d.). Technavio. Retrieved May 22, 2023, from https://analysis.technavio. org/e-learning-industry-analysis-research

This unlocks better and closer friendships and relationships – you will be able to support those you care about far better – and the reputation of being a helpful person worth knowing. Being the person who can cut through the issues at hand and help people discover and choose the correct solution is always invaluable.

No one knows better than a high-ticket closer how little sales have to do with a product. We rarely sell prospects on products, whether we're aiming for a commission or not. When we work our magic, we sell opportunities. We sell potential. We're in the business of selling a better world, and with a gig that good, it's hard to stop selling.

Selling a better life

I met a sad woman at a party. She seemed disinterested as she stood against the wall twirling her wine glass. I walked up to her and said hello, attempting to be friendly. She seemed grateful someone made the effort to approach her.

"So, what do you do?" she asked.

"I'm in high-ticket sales," I said.

"Oh, really?" She asked. She didn't sound impressed. "Do you like it?"

"Yeah, I love it," I smiled.

"What do you like about it?" She took a sip of wine. I paused for a moment to consider my answer.

"I really enjoy helping people find clarity," I said. She was taken aback by my answer.

"I've never heard anyone describe sales that way," her brows furrowed as she looked at me with fascination.

I smiled again. "That's how I see it. But enough about me. What do you do?"

Her disposition changed. She leaned back against the wall.

"I'm a corporate accountant," she hung her head as if she should be ashamed to say it out loud.

"Cool," I said, genuinely. "How long have you been doing that?"

"Ten years," she said.

"Do you enjoy it?"

"Well… it pays very well." She looked off into the distance.

"Honestly, I hate it," she said after a moment. "Sometimes I go to work and I sit at my desk and I think, 'I can't do it. I just can't do it.' I try to read some stupid spreadsheet and it makes me feel physically ill. Even the people in the office. I can't stand them anymore. They're nice people. But… the sight of them is nauseating."

Honestly, I wasn't expecting her to open up this much. She was facing a real emotional problem, and someone needed to guide her to a solution. My instincts kicked in.

"I'm sorry to hear that," I said, "What would you rather do instead?"

"Well…" She looked hopeful for a moment. Then she shook her head. "Oh, I don't know."

"You don't have anything else in mind?"

"My husband and I talked about starting a children's party entertainment business. I love organizing my children's birthday parties, I always get compliments on how great they are, I even often get asked by the other parents if I could organize their own children's parties."

As she spoke about a possible future filled with celebration, young smiling faces, and a chance to do work she was truly passionate about, she stood taller. Her face lit up and she smiled through her sentences.

"I'm sorry," she said, "I've been drinking too much." She waved her hand, dismissing the dream from over her head. "It's just a pipe dream. We could never really do it."

"It sounds like you'd be in a great position to do it," I countered. "You're certainly passionate about it."

She nodded halfheartedly.

"So, what's stopping you from doing it?" I asked. She scoffed.

"It's such a risk," she said. "It would be a massive jump to take."

"That's true," I replied. "But what happens if you don't do it? More miserable days in that office? Listening to your co-workers? Pounding your head against the desk?"

She looked distraught at the thought of this. I tried to cheer her up.

"So, why don't you start working as a party planner on the side?" I suggested. "I'm sure that wouldn't be too hard – you did say you already have some potential clients."

"I just couldn't do that and my corporate job together, I just wouldn't have the time."

I shrugged. "If not that," I said, "where does that leave you?"

She looked out across the party, where people were mingling, drinking, and dancing. I could see her processing years of pain and regret. Then suddenly, she looked at me, a new confidence glistening in her eyes.

"I'm going to quit my job and open a children's party business."

Her eyes widened, surprised by her own words. Then the surprise turned to resolve, and the glistening expression on her face hardened to steely sincerity.

"I have to do this now. If I don't get this business off the ground, I won't have time to start a family like John and I talked about."

I could see her wheels spinning on how she was going to make her dream happen. She hardly noticed as the kinetic energy in her mind yanked her off the wall and away from our corner of the party. I thought she'd disappear, but then she looked back at me and nearly screamed, "Oh my God!"

> "What?" I asked.
>
> "You just mapped out my whole life," she said, incredulous. "How did you do that?"
>
> I smiled and raised my glass toward her. "That's sales".

Discovering the skills of Inverse Closing™ empowers us to nudge others toward change. This is a tremendous power, and as a wise man in a comic book once said, "With great power comes great responsibility!" So, when we're in sales for the right reasons, we can use this power to help ourselves, our prospects, and even strangers make better choices.

We can convince people to uncover their desires, blockages, and considerations around positive life changes. We can sell our loved ones on being better friends and partners. We can help guide anyone toward solutions to the problems that cause them pain.

Economically, mastering sales allows us to grow our businesses exponentially. When we can sell to anyone, our businesses' potential to expand skyrockets. Growing businesses to their full potential with the power of sales means we can take control of our lives and choose where, when, and how we want to work.

We can raise prices, fill our pipelines with new clients, and fill our offices with junior salespeople ready to learn. It grants us the flexibility to choose who we want to work with, rather than desperately filling our agendas with clients we *have* to work with.

Beyond financial success, my Inverse Closing™ approach can rejuvenate the entire concept of "work," transforming it from dreaded to joyous. Implementing Inverse Closing™ provides a sense of progress for salespeople, which is motivational. With this comprehensive system, we gain benchmarks to compare ourselves against. We can track exactly how we're improving and pat ourselves on the back when we reach new heights.

When we realize sales can be a force for good, improving this craft feels especially worthwhile.

It is also a massively useful skill for any job or industry, not just sales. Strong communicative skills set you apart from your competition in any role and set you up for success – when faced between two otherwise identical individuals, the better communicator is always going to win more work or advance further and faster.

How far can these skills go?

As a career, it is true that high-ticket will not make you a millionaire. However, what it does offer you is a comfortable six-figure lifestyle, earning money in the comfort of your own home. This gives you the freedom and flexibility to focus on growing, developing and working on other projects.

As you progress, you get the opportunity to advance vertically – moving up to the higher value deals which can close for anywhere from $50k to $100k, earning higher commissions – or sideways. Advancing sideways involves following in my footsteps by transitioning into a coaching role in which you guide and mentor others into mastering high-ticket sales.

Eventually, this could result in setting up an agency of high-ticket closers. In my case, we currently have 30+ closers working across dozens of different clients.

Honestly, I am so excited to have shared the opportunity to master high-ticket sales with you. It is sincerely the best job I have ever had. Being able to work from the comfort of home and meet all the amazing and lovely people I have calls with – guiding them through their problems – and getting paid a lot of money for it… there are few jobs like it – short of being a rockstar or a professional football player, or similar.

Even with my agency, I still have some clients I do sales for directly – they are top-tier, valuable high-ticket offers and such a pleasure to work for that I can't give them up. In fact, just off three or four of those calls a week, I could make a six-figure salary and live comfortably.

This means that, no matter what the future brings, I can have the security of knowing that I have the skills to guarantee my ability to walk into any organization and be certain that I would be the best closer from day one.

The lessons from this book are powerful because they are shareable. You can use the system outlined here to train others to sell for you. When you adopt this approach, you can treat your sales force as an extraordinary team of elites, with access to knowledge that can lead your business to unseen heights.

Applying the high-ticket sales techniques in this book will improve the world. They will help you build more meaningful relationships inside and outside of work by helping you solve problems for those around you. With these tools in hand, you can achieve greatness and take pride in your title as a high-ticket closer.

So let us go forth embrace the world of high-ticket closing and help rid the world of dodgy sales approaches. Let us leave behind the antiquated tactics that make the everyday person hate salespeople. Instead, let us sell people on changing their lives for the better.

Are you sold?

About the Author

With nearly two decades of experience and an exceptional track record, Adam Cerra is a renowned sales expert and trainer who has personally closed more than $30 million in high-ticket sales throughout his career. Since 2004, he has dedicated his career to mastering the art of high-ticket sales.

Recognized for his innovative approach to high-ticket sales, Adam Cerra is the creator of the revolutionary Inverse Closing Method™. This groundbreaking system, based on Adam's extensive sales experience, combined with his background in neuro-linguistic programming, challenges traditional sales methodologies and provides a fresh perspective on closing high-ticket – transforming the way professionals approach the closing process.

Adam Cerra is not only an accomplished high-ticket closer professional but is also an experienced leader and coach. His extensive experience, innovative strategies, and passion for empowering others makes him a driving force in the high-ticket sales industry – inspiring both individuals and organizations towards success.

Adam's high-ticket sales agency and his highly-trained closers are an invaluable resource for brands offering high-ticket products and services. Some of the biggest brands in the high-ticket space, Paul Mckenna training, Ajit Nawalkha, Mindvalley Inc, Marisa Peer, Jay Shetty Certification school and Peter Sage have benefited significantly from Adam's Inverse Closing Method™, some of whom having seen their sales scale up to seven to eight figures after having outsourced their high-ticket closing to Adam's agency.

In addition, Adam Cerra has excelled in training high-ticket closers though his innovative Cerra Closer Academy™. Using his unique training programs, he has equipped hundreds of sales professionals with the skills and knowledge necessary to succeed in the high-ticket industry.

Resources & Recommendations

I highly recommend joining my Facebook group **High-ticket Revolution - Closing Mastery** where I help you get results with your sales.

Here's what you'll get inside the group:

- Video tear-downs of sales calls

- Q&A videos

- Tips, advice, resources

- Advice on becoming a world-class closer

- Live trainings

- Interviews with entrepreneurs

- Plus so much more!

Join the group here:

Scan me!

By the way, just in case you missed it, if you want additional help in getting the interpretation of your sales call right, then you need my **Inverse Closing Quadrant™**…

It's a complete guide on how to cover all the bases of everything you need to do so you don't lose the sale. All you need to do is scan the QR code below to get it!

Scan me!

World Class High ticket Sales Training

If you want to skyrocket your income as a high-ticket closer and take home an easy 6 figures per year as one of the top 1% of sales closers in the world, then you're in the right place.

My Cerra Closer Academy™ is a 12 week live, hands-on program designed to guide you through my signature Inverse Closing Method™. Unlike other sales programs, you'll get feedback and coaching on real sales calls.

Scan the QR code below to find out more about how my Inverse Closing Method™ can catapult your career like nothing else.

Scan me!

DFY High-Ticket Closing

Want your very own sales team but don't know where to start? I have a complete done-for-you outsourced sales service where my team of elite closers will close calls for you so you can focus on delivering your genius.

If you have an existing team of sales closers and want to ramp up your closing ratio so you can dramatically increase your sales, I can train your team in my signature Inverse Closing Method™.

To find out more, simply visit www.adamcerra.com

Printed in Great Britain
by Amazon